P9-DEE-686

IF YOU CAN JUST GET YOUR
MIND TOGETHER,
THEN COME ACROSS TO ME.
WE'LL HOLD HANDS AND THEN WE'LL WATCH THE SUNRISE FROM THE BOTTOM OF THE SEA.
BUT FIRST, ARE YOU EXPERIENCED?

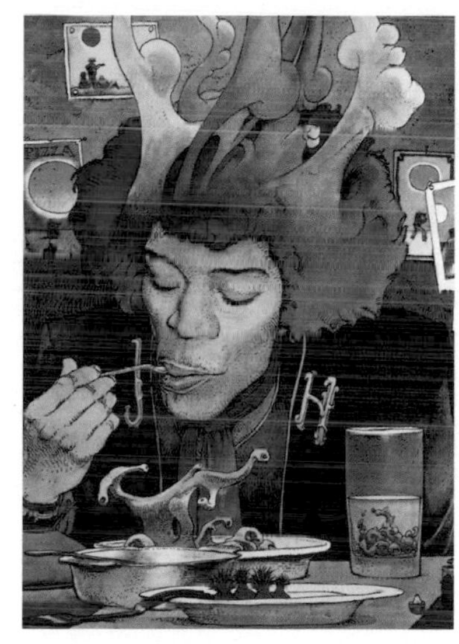

THE ULTIMATE EXPERIENCE

Adrian Boot & Chris Salewicz

Photograph : Gered Mankowitz

THE ULTIMATE EXPERIENCE

Adrian Boot & Chris Salewicz

MACMILLAN • USA

First published in Great Britain in 1995 by Boxtree Limited
Broadwall House
21 Broadwall
London SE1 9PL

MACMILLAN
A Simon & Schuster Macmillan Company
1633 Broadway
New York, NY 10019

A catalogue record is available from the Library of Congress

ISBN 0-02-860836-4

Designed by Stylorouge, London.
Colour reproduction by Fotographics Ltd, London - Hong Kong.
Printed and bound in Italy by de Agostini.

10 9 8 7 6 5 4 3 2 1

This book is dedicated to Al Hendrix and the Hendrix family who continue to keep the spirit of Jimi alive on this earth.

JOHN ADLER JAN BLOOM LAURA BOOMER ADRIAN BOOT RICHARD BULL ED CARAEFF JEAN NOEL COGHE IRA COHEN CAROLINE COON DAVID COSTA MICK FARREN MARK FRENCH and BILL WOOD CAESAR GLEBBEEK RICK GRIFFIN DOUGLAS KENT HALL DEZO HOFFMAN GRAHAM HOWE iQ VIDEOGRAPHICS PROFESSOR GUNTHER KIESER MATI KLARWEIN ALAN KOSS ELLIOTT LANDY JEAN-PIERRE LELOIR LINDA McCARTNEY DAVID MAGNUS GERED MANKOWITZ MOEBIUS MARTIN MONESTIER VICTOR MOSCOSO MICHAEL OCHS ARCHIVES ROB O'CONNOR : STYLOROUGE IVAN OLIVIER RICHARD PETERS MIKE POLILLO DÖLF PREISIG RON RAFAELLI JEAN LOUIS RANCUREL RUSH and BLAM CHRIS SALEWICZ CHARLES SHAAR MURRAY MARTIN SHARP JOSEPH SIA ARNOLD SKOLNIK LUCIA SOLAZZI NEIL SPENCER ROGER STEFFENS WALDEMAR SWIERZY DEREK TAYLOR BRUNO TILLEY ART TROITSKY BERND WEIDEMANN VAL WILMER IAN WRIGHT SUE YOUNG

CONTENTS

NYU
Jimi Hendrix
ON THE ROAD AGAIN
1994
UNIVERSITY TOUR 1994

Purple Haze

This is what happened: during the 1940s a group of ancient souls reincarnated on earth - their purpose was to lead earthlings to a more spiritual course and save the human race from its path towards destruction; in the middle of the 1960s humanity's suicidal behaviour was initially averted as spirituality became materialised in the myriad experiences of an emerging collective higher consciousness.

Jimi Hendrix was in the very top echelons of this soul group, all of whom were strong, fantastic, visionary individuals. The specific purpose of Jimi Hendrix was to set off the violet ray, the seventh ray of colour, the Purple Haze. As we can observe by watching the rainbow that forms around a candle's burning wick, the seventh ray is the last colour before we come truly into the light. When the seventh ray is manifested, we experience the spiritualisation of politics and the breaking down of war karma, something that Jimi in his Martian element was, paradoxically, able to set about fighting. It is a time of high evolutionary cause and effect. And a warrior-angel was sent for this work, a true free spirit who was dedicated to the task of raising the consciousness of this planet. Although such a being often does not last long ...

And on a (sometimes) material plane:

A Chaotic Insight Into Some Of The People Who Have Been Touched By This Project

In addition to the photographers, artists and writers who have contributed directly to this book, many people, over the last few years, during the trauma and excitement of the Jimi Hendrix Ultimate Experience project, have provided support, sympathy, hard work and ideas.

The Jimi Hendrix Ultimate Experience exhibition was researched, designed, produced and toured by Exhibit-A, with the help of Jimi fans and professionals all over this and other planets.

Alan Douglas, master shaman of the project, dedicated himself to ensuring that the exhibition celebrating the work and life of this cosmic emissary would be the finest and most exciting possible. Time and money always seemed to be minor obstacles. Alan, who is also one of the first cyberpunks, was the inspiration and engine behind *The Ultimate Experience*. Everyone at his company, Are You Experienced Inc (AYEI), especially Kyn Sharee and Maxine Martens, was dedicated to the cause and always ready to help. In addition, Bob Tracy was crucial in the design and construction of an immensely complex version of the exhibition: the Ultimate Experience "On The Road Again" tour marked the first time Jimi had toured since 1970. This highly inter-active cyber version was trucked, complete with road crew, around the United States; greatest thanks to tour manager Robert Savene, Michael Monaghan, and Rowland Jung, and to the technical engineer Craig "Hutch" Hutchison; and to Rebanda Transportation, Joe Deandra and Jim Knight, and Speedy Signs, Ukiah, California. And certainly let us not forget the immense assistance of MCA Records in the United States.

It was this Jimi Hendrix exhibition that provided the inspiration for this book. The wealth of material contributed and newly created from around the world was far more than could be included in one volume.

Adrian Boot's co-partner in Exhibit-A, Shelley Warren, earned record air miles shuttling around the world holding together the seemingly impossible logistics of a multiple touring exhibition; formidably dealing with the complex legalities and rights issues as well as making sure everyone stayed on the case and delivered on time. Meanwhile, Lynne Boot, project bursar, made sense of the budgets.

Vicky Fox at Exhibit-A proved a supreme electronic artist, retouching expert, darkroom technician and rock 'n' roll performer.

Neil Storey, Rob Partridge and everyone at the Partridge and Storey office have demonstrated the art of global press coordination. Neil Storey helped us research and write crucial exhibition captions and copy, gave us more high octane midnight oil than anyone else and put up with our bullshit

Rob O'Connor, Richard Bull and Carl Rush for Stylorouge proved far more than the phrase "design house" suggests. exceptionally talented people with extraordinary ideas, inexhaustible enthusiasm, and endless patience. This small design house in west London was the hotbed for the entire project's creative development; they took risks out on the cutting edge of imaging technology that were truly part of a creative endeavour.

Chris Mole, Mike Evans, and Lara von Ahlefeldt and the Screen Ventures team in London were always an invaluable support system. In the United States Kirby Veevers and Sharon Fishman from Veevers Special Events provided vital support, PR and logistical coordinating. Catherine Turner, Chris Kewbank, and Sophie Molins at the Special Photographers Company immediately understood the concept, being the first gallery to show the exhibition. Sebastian Andrews and Charles at Joe's Basement printed and reprinted deep into the night. Pamela Esterson, meanwhile, was an able and dedicated copy editor.

At the highest level of comprehension of Jimi's soul and art Michael Fairchild was the consummate editorial consultant and researcher; Caesar Glebbeek, Jimi's biographer and collector and the editor of the flagship Jimi fanzine *UniVibes*, gave endless support and guidance, equally, so did Bill Nitopi, the Jimi Hendrix collector, writer and expert.

Other great enthusiasts who similarly gave unstintingly of their time and knowledge were Phil Cushway at Artrock, with his posters and encouragement; Jimi collector Ron Thiesen; Michael Ochs at Michael Ochs archives.

How could we forget Christophe Rudier at Gravity in Paris, France? Or Lionel Rotcage, Sandra Propper, Isabelle Lemann, or Nicolo Schluz at Polygram, as well as the able assistance of the FNAC organisation?

Similarly the crucial input of Edward at A Bliss, experts in lamination and display; Chris Parkes, king of merchandising, at MMM, Kevin D'Art at General Framing; Ramus at Island Trading; and Robert Ellis's REP Photographic; and Mike Putland at RETNA Pictures, as well as RLX Features, Redferns, Alchemy, Pictor International, Artomatic, and iQ Videographics.

Gerry Ward and everyone at Anglo Pacific endured all the headaches and hassles of shipping the Jimi exhibition around the world. Richard Edwards at Transeuro also gave his assistance.

In Australasia Fiona Drury at Melbourne's Write Angle impressively coordinated the exhibition. The locations chosen included that in Hobart, Tasmania, Melbourne's Museum of Contemporary Art, Sydney's Australian Centre Of Photography, Brisbane's Cape Gallery, Byron Bay's Long Gallery, Adelaide's State Library, and the Auckland Institute in New Zealand.

Similar international support and assistance above and beyond the call of duty came from Filippo and Angela Passigli and Silvia Salvadori at Idea Books in Milan, Italy; also in Italy, a heartfelt thanks to Luigi Negrini at Kodak. And in Amsterdam, Holland, from Marlene Marcus, Kees van Aardenne, and Bart Jan den Bieman at the remarkable Marcus and Marcus Gallery. And respect to Luis Arbano at Virgin Madrid, Antonio Hidalgo, La Sal Hosteleria Madrid, and Elena Gorostiza at Polygram Spain. Similarly we owe much to Ian Middleton at Ibis Productions in Glasgow in Scotland, and Yvette Lipsey at In The City; to Ted Owen at Bonhams; and to Nigel Glossop at the Portsmouth City Museum, the coolest city museum ever. And to John Stephenson and Gordon Campbell at The Gap in Dublin, whose party no one is capable of remembering.

Rebecka Glaser coordinated the Scandinavian exhibitions, with Peter Alverus in Sweden and Vibeke Christensen at the Sentrum Scene in Oslo; as did Pierre-Jean Critten at Vibrations in Switzerland. The presentation of the Handswerkskammer gallery in Hamburg was impressive, thanks to Klaus Fischer and Mr Hiller, with able assistance from Matthias Schultz, Michael Eberhardt, Brigit Schmuser and Carola Spuling of Polydor Germany. Thanks also to Joachim W Schiwy in Berlin, and Theresa Bergne, Andre Feldmann and Arne Schultchen.

In Ljubljana, Slovenia, cultural pundit Marko Prpic coordinated and produced the exhibition; with Mira Semic of Art Spedal's sterling back-up. In Argentina Teresa Rojas and Menena Garces de Mosto of Mosto y Rojas/Texo coordinated and produced the exhibition at the Centro Cultural de la Cuidad de Buenos Aires, with help from Ernie Reid at Polygram Argentina.

Among many others in the United States, we are deeply grateful to John Mullane at Transcom, Chris Murray at Washington's Govinda Gallery, Bruce Clements at Excalibur in Chicago, and to Richard Flanzer from InVision, as well as to Glen Rabbach at Duggal Color Projects, Ben Hartley at Ruder Finn, and Alvenia Bridges for insight and PR.

Much respect also to Don Letts, dread film-maker and friend, Jim Marshall, Barry Wentzell, John Van Hammersveld, Cally, Peter Sanders, David Byrd, Frank Kozic, Chris Craske, Weine Lexius, Bob Cummings, Bill Seinkiewicz, George Shuba, Frank Gauna, Jim Cummins, Dave Sygall, Tom Hammang, Donald Silverstein, Mick Haggerty, Michael Putland, Robbie Montgomery and Zoe Metcalfe at Linda's Photo Library, Ben Valkhoff, Shelley's mother and father, DHL, Leo Branton Jr, Dexter, Felix Boot, Julian from Highland Printing, Linda Saville, Timothy White, Niall Stokes, Bill Graham, Michael Havas, and Camera Press in London. And to the following at Polygram in its various territories: David Munns, Chris Griffin, Barry French, Jackie Stansfield and Fay at Polygram International in London; Adam Holt in Australia; Milan Herman in the Czech Republic; Kjeld Stefansen in Denmark; Charlie Solomon in Israel; Elii Tofollo in Italy; Eivind Slotsvik in Norway; Luis Busch in Spain; Marko Soderstom in Sweden; Henk Keuter in Holland.

Also ever present and on the vibe were Kathy Etchingham, Monika Danneman, Chas Chandler, Chris Charlesworth, Cosmic Tim, and Glen Colson. And how could we omit the sterling aid and guidance of Boxtree, especially Humphrey Price and Clare Hulton, whom we met through the able steering of our needs by Julian Alexander, our estimable agent.

Any attempt to list all those people that have contributed to the project over the years would be impossible without committing grave errors. The editors of this book and Exhibit-A, the exhibition organisers, would like to apologise for any omissions. No one is worth more than anyone else.

(1942)

I remember a nurse putting a diaper on me and almost sticking me. I must have been in the hospital sick about something, because I remember I didn't feel so good. Then she took me out of this crib and held me up to the window, and she was showing me something up against the sky. It was fireworks and all that, so it must have been the 4th of July. That nurse turned me on, being high on penicillin she probably gave me, and I was looking up and the sky was just ... ssschuusssSchush! Our first trip there ...

Photograph : Ron Rafaelli / Michael Ochs Archives

I WRITE A LOT OF WORDS ALL OVER T

MATCHBOXES, OR

ANYWHERE. SOMETIMES THE MUSIC COMES

WHEN I'M SITTING ARO

NOTHING,

I'M NOT AND THEN THE MUSIC MAKES

ME THINK OF A FEW WORDS

ASHAMED

TO SAY I CAN'T WRITE NO HAPPY SONGS.

FOXY LADY IS ABOUT THE ONLY HAPP

I DON'T FEEL VERY HAPPY WHEN I START WRITING.

I WANT TO TURN PEOPLE ON AND L

HAPPENING.

THAT'S MY REASON FOR BEING AROUND,

AND THE ONLY WAY

I CAN EXPLAIN MYSELF THOROUGHL

IN MUSIC YOU'VE GOT TO SAY SOMETHING REAL JUST

THAT'S THE IDEA OF IT. MAKE IT

I DON'T MEAN MY LYRICS TO BE C

I JUST SAY WHAT I FEEL

FIGHT OVER IT,

IF IT'S INTERESTING ENOUGH.

Photograph : Ron Rafaelli / Michael Ochs Archives

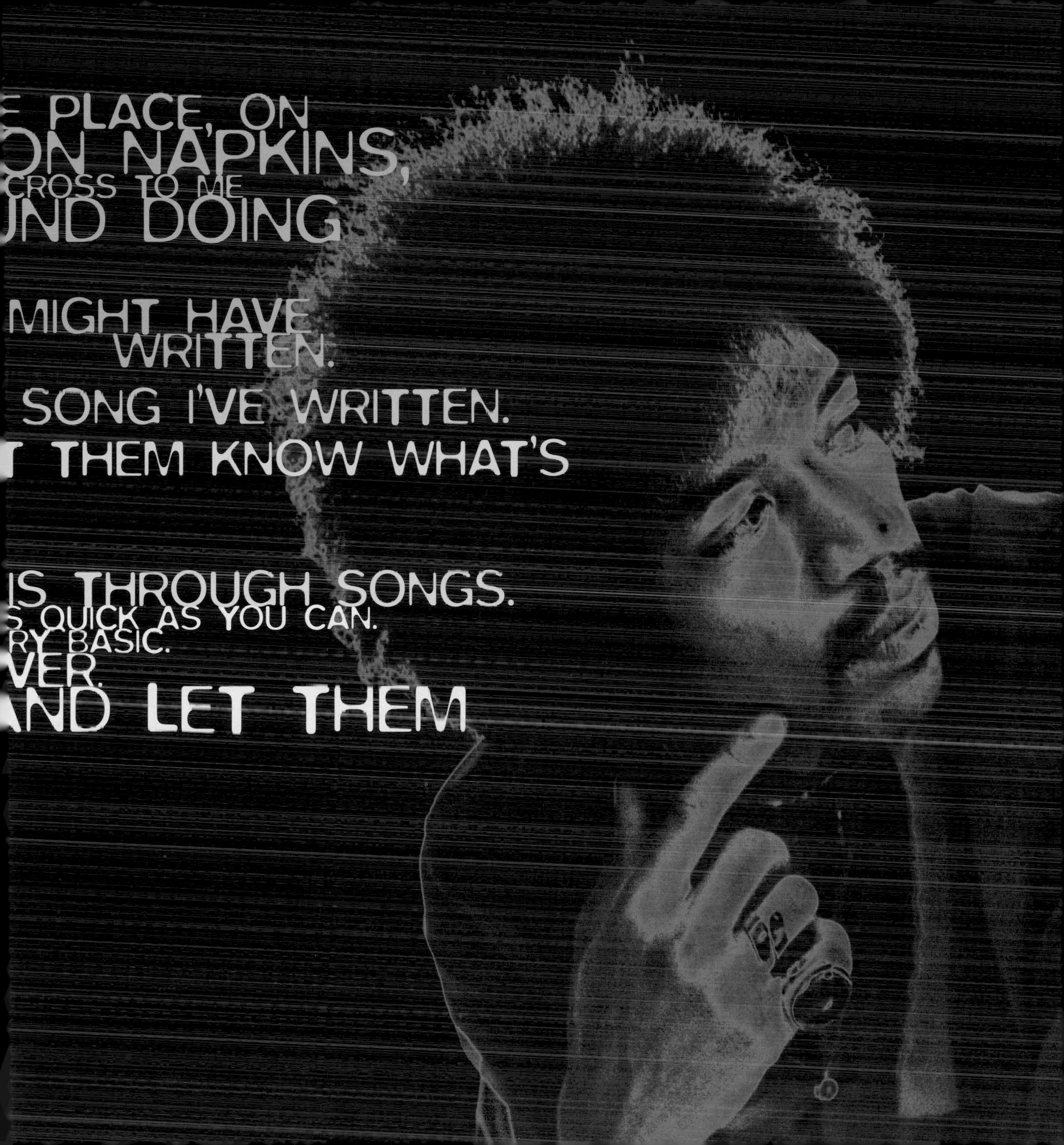

E PLACE, ON
ON NAPKINS,
CROSS TO ME
UND DOING

MIGHT HAVE
WRITTEN.

SONG I'VE WRITTEN.

T THEM KNOW WHAT'S

IS THROUGH SONGS.
S QUICK AS YOU CAN.
RY BASIC.
VER.
AND LET THEM

Born At The Age Of Zero (1992)
Art : Ian Wright

"When I first started I was largely influenced by the blues artists. I just listened to the way people played blues guitar and I dug it. Blues to me means Elmore James, Howlin' Wolf, Muddy Waters and Robert Johnson. You can have your own blues. Everyone has some kind of blues to offer."

"I can't tell you the number of times it hurt me to play the same notes, the same beat. I wanted my own scene, making my own music. I always had a feeling that, if my mind was right, I'd get a break some day. It took a long time, playing a lot of dates that didn't pay very well but I figured it was worth it. I don't think I could have stood another year of playing behind people. I'm glad Chas rescued me."

"I am you searching to be free..."

In the early morning Cherokee mist Jimi is a horseman riding across the plains, a Native American witch-doctor, a shaman. Around his pinto pony run a herd of blue-grey, spirit-like horses...

In the 1950s the western world finally moves out of the nineteenth century ... with an atomic bang straight into the second half of the twentieth. Post-war greyness and Victorian morality and thinking are blasted apart by television, by sputniks, by relative affluence (for some, mainly middle class and white), and most of all by rhythm'n'blues and rock'n'roll ... by the unbelievable Elvis Presley and his pink Cadillac; by Chuck Berry with his pimp's patent leather hair and duckwalk and street poems; by Little Richard's fundamentalist tunes and his bizarre, confrontational beauty; by the hedonist of heaven and hell, Jerry Lee Lewis. Pumped up by a story-hungry mass media – with a cynical, dismissive tone? who cares: what do they know! – there has been nothing like this before. The impact is extraordinary: suddenly there is hope, there is a point to life. Out on art's slicing edge, bohemia is as brave, as poets, painters and jazz musicians search out the cosmic details of their souls.

When he is sixteen, in 1958, Jimi Hendrix is given his first guitar. It has cost five dollars. In some ways it is a substitute for Lucille, his prodigal mother, who has died earlier in the year, on February 2, from cirrhosis of the liver.

Jimi is born in Seattle, Washington, on November 27, 1942. As is the case with many black families in the United States, his upbringing has its religious side: in the Pentecostal church attended by his father he observes and begins to take part in the holy dancing and music, the songs of praise that are forever being changed and rearranged. At home his life is lived out to a soundtrack of the blues, his father being the proud owner of a classic record collection.

> *I remember when I was only four and I wet my pants and I stayed out in the rain for hours so I would get wet all over and my mom wouldn't know. She knew though.*

But who is Jimi's mother? The cirrhosis of the liver that kills her, a testament to her lifestyle, painfully illustrates what she considers her priorities. Lucille Jeter is a wild woman of the night, devoted to having a good time. Before she has lived out enough of her fantasies she finds herself pregnant by Al Hendrix at the age of seventeen (he is six years older than her) – a baby having a baby. Too young an age to have a child, especially for a woman who loves liquor and staying up all night dancing and smooching with men – not that she would let being pregnant with Jimi get in the way of her devotion to having a good time. So this party girl with her erratic, dysfunctional energies, the personification of the absent mother, is Jimi's first female archetype, the template for his understanding of women. From a very young age Jimi starts to have some very blasting experiences. Getting knocked about like that when you're a young child breaks you or makes you.

> *Dad was level-headed and religious, but my mother used to like having a good time and dressing up. She used to drink a lot and didn't take care of herself, but she was a groovy mother. There were family troubles between my mother and father. They used to break up all the time and I always had to be ready to go tippy-toeing off to Canada. My brother and I used to go to different homes. I stayed mostly at my aunt's and grandmother's.*
>
> *My grandmother's a full-blooded Indian, that's all. I used to spend a lot of time on her reservation in British Columbia. There's a lot of them on the reservation, man, and it was really terrible. Every single house is the same, and it's not even a house, it's like a hut ...*
>
> *Yeah, my grandma is full-blooded Cherokee. She used to tell me beautiful Indian stories, and the kids at school would laugh when I wore the shawls and poncho things she made ... There's a lot of people in Seattle that have Indian mixed in them. It's just another part of our family, that's all.*

Lucille comes back to Jimi in dreams; after one he writes the song "Angie".

Often thought of as a love song, "Angie" in fact reveals Jimi's fantasy of his mother returning to earth to collect her son – with all the poetic, prescient sub-text that lies lurking there. On some of the early demos for that song, Jimi sings the line, "And she said little boy …"

In the song "Belly-button Window", meanwhile, Jimi is speaking at a spiritual level, with great objectivity, to both his parents. An extraordinary concept, Jimi recalls how this existence appeared to him as an embryo in his mother's womb, looking out of her "belly-button window"; he asks if his parents really want him around; if they don't, he says, he vows not to return to earth any more.

A quiet child, who more and more reveals an imagination of startling originality, Jimi knows how to listen. He learns to speak only when he has something to say, which will often be encapsulated in just one sentence he will drop into a conversation.

The errant ways of Jimi's mother drive his father nuts.

> *My dad was very strict and taught me that I must respect my elders always. I couldn't speak unless I was spoken to first by grown-ups. So I've always been very quiet. But I saw a lot of things.*
>
> *I used to be really lonely. I used to bring a stray dog home every night till my pa let me keep one.*

Trying to keep his boys on the straight and narrow, bringing them up the best way he knows for them to survive … Lucille's erratic entries and exits from his sons' lives are distractions from his best efforts at establishing some order for them. And they hardly display her as a dependable role model. Al Hendrix soldiers on: redoubling the effort to imbue his boys with various cardinal virtues: politeness, generosity, for example. In their turn, however, his sons feel hard done by that their father makes them do labouring work on his various projects for no pay. All he is trying to do, however, is ensure that, most of the time at least, there will be food on the table … But a lot of the time they are, frankly, poverty-stricken. Later, when Lucille dies early in 1958, Al refuses to allow the children to attend her funeral, unleashing an abrasive resentment.

> *There's some dream I had when I was real little; like my mother being carried away on these camels, and it was a big caravan and you can see the shade, the leaf patterns across her face – you know how the sun shines through a tree, well these were green and yellow shadows. And she's saying, "Well, I won't be seeing you too much any-more, you know, so I'll see you." And about two years after that she died … There's some dreams you never forget.*

> *Dad was a gardener and he'd once been an electrician. We had to carry stones and cement all day and he pocketed the money.*

Jimi grows up listening to iconic inspirations from his father's collection: from Elmore James and Muddy Waters to Howlin' Wolf and BB King. By the time he reaches his teens, Jimi has also discovered the primal magic of early rock'n'roll and r&b, and begins to learn the guitar by practising along to the hot tunes of the day. Before he has an instrument of his own, he plays with a broom handle; then he attaches a piece of wood to a large cigar-box.

The teenage Jimi Hendrix is a great fan of Elvis Presley. On September 1, 1957, he goes to see Elvis play at Seattle's Sicks Stadium, the king of rock'n'roll at his prime for the fourteen-year-old boy. That same year Little Richard (who has had a big hit with a song whose title is the same as Jimi's mother's name – Lucille) comes to Seattle to see his mother who lives in the city – during a tour of Australia Little Richard has decided that he should henceforth do only the Lord's work and has flown back to the States. His mother has a place just round the corner from Jimi and his younger brother Leon, and she knows the boys are just nuts about music. So she sends round Little Richard, in penitent mood, to see them in his Cadillac. The brothers are bemused. An old bluesman lives nearby. And Jimi will go and watch him play, sitting out on his stoop of a hot summer evening; he observes how he runs his fingers over the frets, uplifted despite his age and the oppression lines on his face as he pulls the country blues tunes from deep within him.

About Jimi there is always a strange sense of certainty, of knowing the unknown. As he develops a fondness for reading, Jimi learns that these sensations and vibrations of the strange, angular, and poetic take form and shape in the science fiction that he comes to love. Flash Gordon is Jimi's favourite character. At school in Seattle this nervous pupil, whose stuttering exposes his sensitivity, paints pictures of life on Jupiter, the planet that astrologers will advise is a harbinger of good fortune.

> *At school I used to write poetry a lot and then I was really happy. My poems were mostly about flowers and nature and people wearing robes. I wanted to be an actor or a painter. I particularly liked to paint scenes on other planets. Summer Afternoon On Venus, and stuff like that. The idea of space travel excited me more than anything else.*
>
> *They said I used to be late all the time, but I was getting As and Bs. The real reason was I had a girl-friend in the art class and we used to hold hands all the time. The art teacher didn't dig that at all. She was very prejudiced. She said, "Mr Hendrix, I'll see you in the cloakroom in three seconds, please." In the cloakroom she said, "What do you mean, talking to that white woman like that?" I said, "What are you, jealous?" She started crying and I got thrown out. I cry easy.*

The death of his mother marks a watershed. Jimi's true love becomes his guitar, and during the summer vacation of 1959 he begins to work with a variety of bands in his home town. He is impressed with a tenor sax player called Big Jay McNeely who plays his instrument lying on his back; as a consequence, Jimi tried to make his guitar sound like a saxophone. He plays with the Velvetones and various other Seattle groups before moving on to the Rocking Kings, formed by a high school friend. The group show promise, even claiming second place in the All State Band Of The Year contest in Seattle during 1960.

> *I always dug string instruments and pianos, but I wanted something I could take home or anywhere … Then I started digging guitars.*
>
> *When it was time for us to play on stage I was all shaky, so I had to play behind the curtains. I just couldn't get up in front. And then you get so very discouraged. You hear different bands playing around you and the guitar player always seems like he's so much better than you are. Most people give up at this point, but it's best not to. Just keep on, just keep on. Sometimes you are going to be so frustrated you'll hate the guitar, but all of this is just a part of learning. If you stick with it you're going to be rewarded. If you're very stubborn you can make it.*

Pretty soon they begin playing regular gigs as far away as Vancouver, sixty miles to the north. Half the group eventually quit, however, and the remaining band members re-form under the name Thomas and the Tomcats.

Jimi is particularly fond of Muddy Waters, who makes the first serious impact on him of any musician.

> *The first guitarist I was aware of was Muddy Waters. I heard one of his records when I was a little boy and it scared me to death, because I heard all those sounds. Wow! What was that all about? It was great. I liked Muddy Waters when he had only two guitars, harmonica and bass drum. Things like "Rollin" and "Tumblin" were what I liked – that real primitive guitar sound.*

As well as BB King, Elmore James and Howlin' Wolf, he is soon also into Jimmy Reed, John Lee Hooker and Roscoe Gordon. He has noted, meanwhile, the way that Charlie Patton plays his guitars behind his head, as does Tommy Johnson.

Girls come calling, but Jimi tells his father to say he isn't at home. Rather than a sign of great moral certainty, however, this is simply a reflection of Jimi's habitual shyness. Meanwhile, on

Big Red (1960/61). Photograph : Al Hendrix

*"Mostly my dad took care of me. He was a gardener but we weren't too rich. It got pretty bad in the winter when there wasn't any grass to cut.
My first instrument was a harmonica."*

Jimi posing with his red-painted Danelectro outside his house at 2606 Yesler Way in Seattle. The night before, Jimi had played with the Tomcats and bandleader Perry Thomas had charged him $5.00 hire for his jacket. As usual, the cash had to be handed over - along with the jacket - the morning after each show.

nights out with his friends a wildness is raising its head that can result in big problems. In fact, it is beginning to look like music or jail: in May 1961 Jimi is arrested for being in a car that has been taken without the owner's consent.

> *I was eighteen. I didn't have a cent in my pocket. I spent seven days in the cooler for taking a ride in a stolen car. But I never knew it was stolen.*

Two days later he is arrested again for taking another vehicle. He is only saved from a custodial sentence when his lawyer assures the judge that his client is considering joining the army. The sentence? Two years, suspended, but get your ass down to that recruitment office now. He does. And after basic training he goes on to Paratrooper School; he graduates in January 1962 to become a "Screaming Eagle", a parachutist in the 101st Airborne.

Based at Fort Campbell in Kentucky, Jimi is able literally to float in space, at one with the cosmos until his feet hit the ground.

> *When you first jump it's really outasight … You're just there at the door and all of a sudden, FLOP! RUSH! For a split second a thought went through me like, You're crazy! … It's so personal, because once you get out there everything is so quiet. All you hear is the breeze … It's the most alone feeling in the world … Then you feel that tug on your collar … And so you look up and there's that big, beautiful, white mushroom above you. That's when you begin talking to yourself again, and you just say, "Thank the Lord". That was about the best thing in the army – the parachute drops. I did about twenty-five.*

Back on earth at the military base he is unable to float through life so freely as when he is dangling on a parachute. The local radio stations are immersed in the blues and southern r&b, but Jimi's musical obsession, coupled with his introverted nature, provoke open hostility from his fellow soldiers – comments are made by Jimi's barrack-mates when he sleeps with his guitar. He spends much of his free time in nearby Nashville, hanging out in the town's myriad music clubs.

> *The army's really a bad scene. They wouldn't let me have anything to do with music. They tell you what you are interested in, and you don't have any choice.*

Dream time is very important to Jimi, and there is little head space for sensitive self-nurturing in the daily military routine. However, he does make one invaluable ally while in the army. Stationed at the same army camp is another soldier with musical inclinations, a bass player called Billy Cox; he and Jimi become friends, and start playing together; they form a group called the King Kasuals: they play not only the service lounges but also off-base clubs. This is the only part of his army life in which Jimi can find fulfilment. So after he breaks his ankle during one drop, Jimi plays the injury card and gets himself invalided out of the US army.

> *One morning I found myself standing outside the gate of Fort Campbell on the Tennessee-Kentucky border with my little duffle bag and three or four hundred dollars in my pocket. I was going back to Seattle which was a long way away. But there was this girl I was kinda hung up on.*

Waiting around Kentucky until Billy Cox also leaves the service … Then Jimi and the bass player move to Nashville, keeping the King Kasuals going. They begin touring the "chitlin" circuit, the black showbusiness network of southern bars, theatres and clubs. "Chitlin" is a corruption of chitterling, pigs' intestines, the cheapest meat, a staple of soul food. And they are considered cheap meat, these acts playing the circuit: it is an uncomfortable hand-to-mouth existence in the King Kasuals. Like many of the other guitarists playing these same southern venues, as well as those anxious to grasp a crowd's attention in the sweaty clubs of southside Chicago, Jimi will play his guitar behind his back or pick his guitar strings with his teeth; such instrumental acrobatics have their origins in the similar performances of African musicians, talking drummers who will play with their instruments behind their backs or standing on their heads, for example.

> *I started a group called the Kasuals with a fellow who played funky, funky bass [Billy Cox]. It was pretty tough at first. I was often in a situation where I didn't know where my next meal was coming from.*

> *I used to have a childhood ambition to stand on my own feet, without being afraid to get hit in the face if I went into a white restaurant and ordered a white steak. But normally I just didn't think along these lines. I had more important things to do – like playing guitar.*

> *I like Robert Johnson. He's so cool. That sort of music gets the message over and comes through so easily.*

> *There used to be cats playing behind their heads or playing with their teeth or elbows ... Some cat tried to get me to play behind my head because I would never move too much. I said, "Oh man, who wants to do all that junk?" ... The idea of playing guitar with my teeth came to me in a town in Tennessee. Down there you have to play with your teeth or else you get shot.*

In the winter of 1962 Jimi moves to Vancouver where he has a regular gig with a local band called, with a certain sense of civic pride, the Vancouvers (featuring, incidentally, as lead vocalist one Tommie Chong, later to become half of the comedy duo, Cheech and Chong).

Jimi returns south at the start of 1963. In Atlanta, in need of musicians, Little Richard, who has reconsidered his promise to the Lord to give up rock'n'roll, hires half the band with whom Jimi is then working; the deal includes their guitar player. Jimi is to remain with Little Richard for a considerable time, playing not only live dates but also on studio sessions. Although Richard's finest moments have come in the preceding decade it seems inevitable to suggest he is a primary influence on the young guitarist; the singer's flamboyance and sheer stage presence make a significant impression.

> *He wouldn't let us wear frilly shirts on stage. Once me and Glyn Wildings got some fancy shirts because we were tired of wearing the uniform. After the show, Little Richard said, "Brothers, we've got to have a meeting. I'm Little Richard and I'm the King of Rock and Rhythm and I'm the only one who's going to look pretty on stage. Glyn and Jimi, will you please turn in those shirts or else you will have to suffer the consequences of a fine." He had another meeting over my hairstyle. I said I wasn't going to cut my hair for nobody. That was another five dollar fine. If* our *shoelaces were two different types we'd get fined another five bucks. Everybody on the tour was brainwashed.*

> *Little Richard: I first met Jimi Hendrix in Atlanta, Georgia, where he was stranded with no money. He had been working as a guitarist with a feller called Gorgeous George ... Jimi was staying in this small hotel. And so he came by to see us. He had watched me work and just loved the way I wore those headbands around my hair and how wild I dressed ... So he came with me. He wasn't playing my kind of music, though. He was playing like BB King, blues. He started rocking though and he was a good guy. He began to dress like me and even grew a little moustache like mine.*

Despite his time on the road, Jimi has no real reputation at all: he is simply another guitar player trying to scrape a living, another hired gun. But he is learning the essence of stagecraft. Gigs, however, are hard to find, although there is one fan, a friend of Ronnie Isley. Ronnie is a member of the Isley Brothers who, a few years earlier, smashed the charts with such hits as "Twist And Shout" and "Shout". The group is looking for a guitar player and Ronnie's friend, who has seen Jimi at an audition, recommends him. The result is regular work with the Isleys who appreciate him and – less uptight than other soul acts and r&b acts – even allow Jimi to take the occasional solo spot, an invaluable experience. And he really learns soul music.

Jimi is alive with ideas about stretching the guitar to the max. Such explorations, however, have never been accommodated in his previous bands; the guitarist's function in r&b is to follow the singer, embellish the melody lines but never to take the upfront space. But despite his rising reputation with the Isley Brothers, Jimi is still not satisfied.

Photograph : Douglas Kent Hall

“. . .down there you have to play

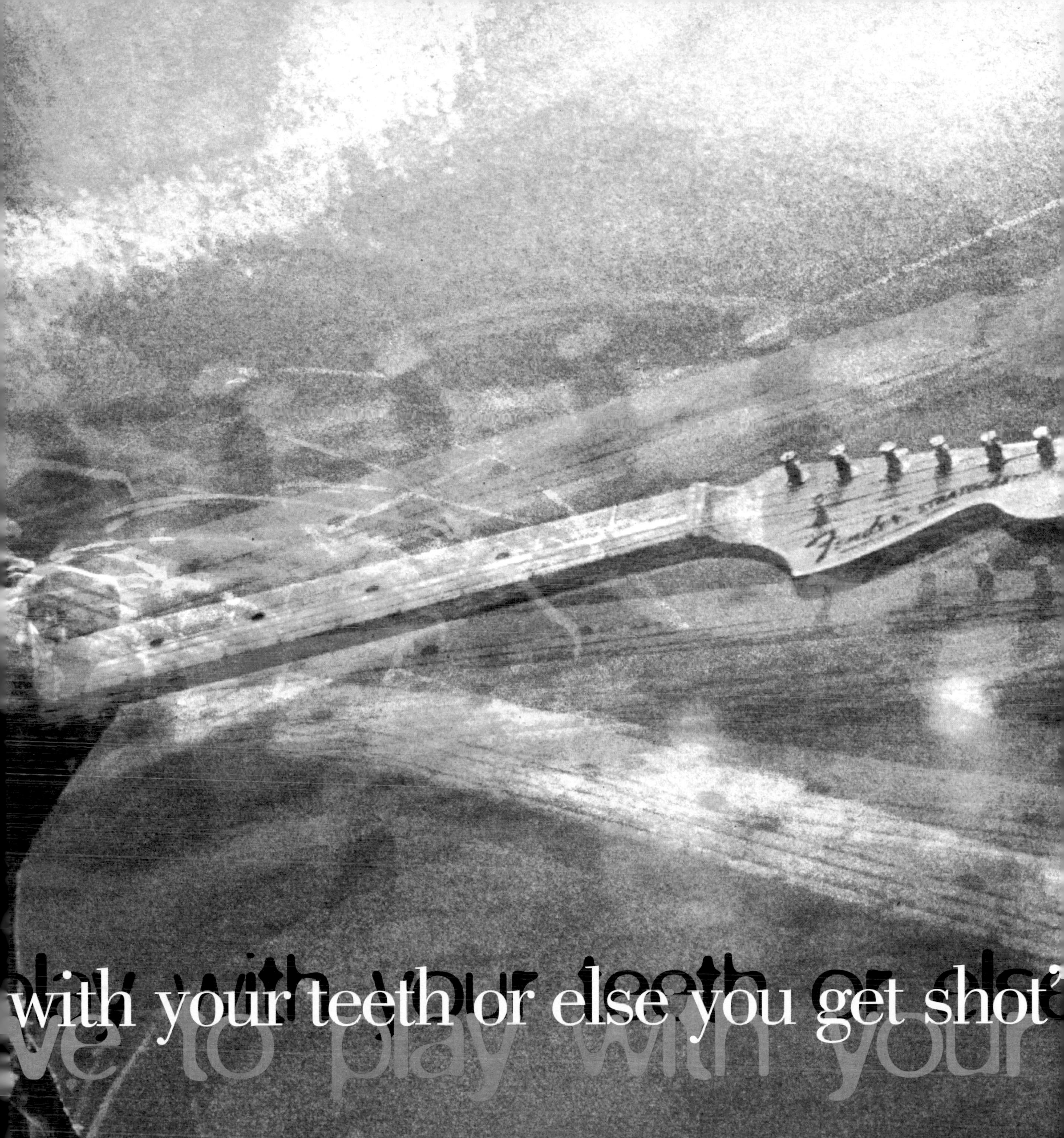
with your teeth or else you get shot'
ve to play with your

"In Nashville I met a guy called Gorgeous George and he got me on some tours. The idea of playing the guitar with my teeth came to me in a town in Tennessee. Down there you have to play with your teeth or else you get shot. There's a trail of broken teeth all over every stage in the South. I understand some guy tried in a club the other night and lost three teeth. They don't know the secret of my success, clean living."

Previous page : A Paintbox manipulation by Richard Baker of Ron Rafaelli's original, taken at Bakersfield Coliseum on October 26, 1968.

Photograph : Michael Ochs Archives

original, taken at Bakersfield Coliseum on October 26th, 68.

Photograph : Linda McCartney

It's not an act, but a state of being. I play and move as I feel. My music, my instrument, my sound, my body, are all one action with my mind.

The song "The Wind Cries Mary" is nothing but a story about a break-up, just a girl and a boy breaking up, that's all... It was recorded in about two takes... We never do more than five or six takes in a recording studio, it's too expensive.

Before I came to England I was digging a lot of the things Bob Dylan was doing. When I first heard him I thought, you must admire the guy for having that much nerve to sing so out of key. But then I started listening to the words. He is giving me inspiration. Not that I want to sound like him - I just want to sound like Jimi Hendrix - but you have to write your own songs in order to get your own personal sound.

When I was in Britain I used to think about America every day. I'm American. I wanted people here to see me. I also wanted to see whether we could make it back here.

You're not a love-in person just because you have curly hair or wear bells and beads. You have to believe in it, not just throw flowers.

Music is very serious to me. Other people may think it's a load of junk or senseless, but it's my way of saying what I want to say. My own thing is in my head. I hear sounds and if I don't get them together, nobody else will

Tokpela : Th

The first world was To
But first, they say, the

All else was endless space. There was no beginning and no end,
had its beginning and end, time, shape, and life in the mind of

ed Sotuknang to make it manifest, saying to him, "I have created
out my plan for life in endless space. I am your Uncle. You are
r order so they may work harmoniously with one another

First World

pace he gathered that which was to be manifest as solid
ine universal kingdoms: one for Taiowa the Creator, one for
this, Sotuknang went to Taiowa and asked, "Is this according to

the same thing with the waters. Place them on the surfaces of
and each."
was to be manifest as the waters and placed them on the
going now to Taiowa, he said, "I want you to see the work I

put the forces of air into peaceful movement about all."
hat which was to be manifest as the airs, made them into great
ents around each universe.
ording to my plan, Nephew. You have created the universes and
them in their proper places. But your work is not yet finished.
the four parts, Túwaqachi, of my universal plan."

commanded. From endless space he gathered that which was to be manifest as solid
s, and arranged them into nine universal kingdoms: one for Taiowa the Creator, one for
for the life to come. Finishing this, Sotuknang went to Taiowa and asked, "Is this
owa. "Now I want you to do the same thing with the waters. Place them on the surfaces
ll be divided equally among all and each."
om endless space that which was to be manifest as the waters and placed them on the
be half solid and half water. going now to Taiowa, he said, "I want you to see the work
ou."
wa. "The next thing now is to put the forces of air into peaceful movement about all."
endless space he gathered that which was to be manifest as the airs, made them into
em into the gentle ordered movements around each universe.
have done a great work according to my plan, Nephew. You have created the universes
olids, waters, and winds, and put them in their proper places. But your work is not yet

First World

ela (Endless Space).
was only the Creator, Taiowa. A
no shape, no life. Just an
nd life in the mind of Taiowa t

nang to make it manifest, sayin
son, to carry out my plan for lif
d lay out these universes in pro
to my plan.

gathered that which was to be
them into nine universal kingdor
for the life to come. Finishing t
plan?"
e thing with the waters. Place
ong all and each.
be manifest as the waters and
water, going now to Taiowa, he

forces of air into peaceful mo

was to be manifest as the air
movements around each unive
my plan, Nephew. You have c
s, and put them in their proper
s movement to complete the fo

Photograph : Graham Howe / Camera Press
Backstage at the Roundhouse in London on February 22, 1967.

Art : Bernd Weidermann

What is perfect?

Perfect is death.

Termination.

It's a physical death.

And after death is the end and the beginning.

There's no telling how many lives your spirit will go through,

die and be reborn.

Art : Bernd Weidermann

Photograph : Jean-Pierre Leloir

THE SEXIEST MAN THAT'S WALKED THE PLANET

"To me Jimi Hendrix was the first black man whose sexuality was relentless and allowed to exist. I remember being really young - around seven or eight - and being fascinated by his persona; even at that age I found his sexual energy to be extremely powerful.

"So many black artists were either great singers or great dancers, but they didn't combine those factors in that extremely sexual way. Even James Brown had great energy, but without that sexuality.

"One of the things I found fascinating about Jimi Hendrix was that uninhibited sexuality. I remember being in a car where we lived in Hicksville, Sweden, outside a shopping centre called Bestro. My father, Don Cherry, came out and told me that Jimi had died. I can still remember sitting in the car and feeling the sadness and shock of being told about it. Don, who knew him a little bit, told me that Jimi walked sideways, like the coolest man on the planet. Don used to bump into him from time to time in Stockholm.

"So many of my memories of him have these mystical overtones in any picture that I have of him. I've just listened to that song 'Drifting', and you can hear how in the later stuff he stepped into another groove. There are certain things that are timeless and will always remain relevant. I think it's really important that he wasn't making music just to fit one genre. And he was definitely the sexiest man that's walked the planet."

Neneh Cherry

Photograph : Joel Axelrad / Retna

I feel very guilty whe
say I'm the greatest
around. What's good
doesn't matter to me
how you feel about w
you're doing that ma

I like the guitar best. It's part of me now guitar that I'm interested in. It's my mus talk through music anyway. Maybe if I ge probably get something together.

Michael Ochs Archives

Jamming is kind of like making love to one another musically.

The Star Spangled Banner (1968)

As photographer Rafaelli remembers it, this six-image print is of Jimi's right hand caught in the act of deconstructing the American National Anthem, The Star Spangled Banner, in Hawaii. Jimi recorded his variant on the theme in March 1969 but it had been a highlight of his sets since the previous year - the first time it was played live was in Columbia, Maryland on August 16th, 1968.

Oh say, does that Star Spangled Banner yet wave
O'er the land of the free
And the home of the brave
Francis Scott Key (1812)

people
But it's not necessarily
I'm trying to get across, I
uitarist
my guitar together, I'll
or bad
It's
Like painting a picture together.
nat
ers

I think this hairstyle is groovy. It's better than having dull, straight hair. The strands, you see, are vibrations. If your hair is straight and pointing to the ground you don't get many vibrations. This way, though, I've got vibrations shooting out all ways..

My dad was very strict and taught me that I must respect my elders always. I couldn't speak unless I was spoken to first by grown-ups. So I've always been very quiet. But I saw a lot of things.

I used to be really lonely. I used to bring a stray dog home every night till my pa let me keep one.

I can't stay in one place too long. It drags me down, regardless of what's happening. I'm scared of vegetating. I have to move on. There's so much to see and so many places to go. I wish I could travel all the time.

I like to consider myself timeless. After all, it's not how long you've been around or how old you are that matters; it's how many miles you've travelled.

It's the physical and emotional toll I have to think of. You go somewhere, the show is a bit under what it should be and you are told you are slipping... but it's the strain. It's the strain of the moral obligation to keep going, even when you don't feel that you can manage even one more show.

There's other moves I have to make now, a little more towards a spiritual level through music.

Shot in Miami at the Castaway Hotel during a break in the two day Miami Pop Festival, May 18-19 1968, which was held at the Gulf Stream Race Track close to Miami Beach. Twenty thousand came to see the Experience headline over Mothers Of Invention, Chuck Berry and John Lee Hooker for which the finale was a forty foot high peace symbol blazing in the night sky. However, that was about all that blazed apart from tempers. Much of the second day and all of the third was lost due to torrential storms: nobody wanted to play for fear of electrocution.

Photograph : Linda McCartney

It was Stella, my lucky star Stella, who – one starstudded and crispy night in lower Manhattan – brought Jimi Hendrix down to my loft to see and look (and gape)at my newly finished temple of love and madness.

As soon as Jimi entered my painted cubicle, the nonchalantly swaying fringes of his Moroccan hippy-superstar jacket stiffened like frozen stalactites and his kinky hair straightened out with the sound of a million liberated bedsprings. He stayed in there for a long time in silence (that special Jimi Hendrix silence). Then his thoughts came pouring out his lush lips in that voice that always seemed to come from the other side of the tunnel of awareness: "The painting I most identify with is the … is the, uhm … the one that looks like a horizontal eight with the two melting Picasso faces inside the rings representing eternity that feels like me when I play myself out too far with the music."

"It represents the 8th Avatar of Vishnu slipping through the keyhole linking the 2x4 dimensions we enter before being born on the ninth month of pregnancy which is for Vishnu the dwarf or baby Avatar, and the tenth is the horse and rider merging into one single Buddha energy of pure and holistic awareness enlightenment beyond life and change," I added.

"I want to be, and maybe am there," Jimi replied. "I don't spend time counting my cents because it makes sense not to be slowed down by the dollar religion of these Solid States of America, hey – they can have it all … know what I'm sayin'?"

Well, not exactly all; he did have an ongoing love affair with his enormous audience, but his earnings were all funnelled away into the pockets of his managers, agents, enchufados and chupadores. His conversation kept slipping and sliding on the banana peels of his basic shyness, his voice would trail off into a hidden horizon and then return like a shortwave radio station from Tasmania.

My guru Paul the Greek used to say, "Every living cell wants to do two things, to preserve and to expand,

and awareness is the symptom of such a schizophrenic tension."

And it was precisely that tension between the expansion of his mind and the retention of his immense popularity that made his inner chords snap.

I had a clear vision of it one night when we went to his benefit concert at Madison Square Garden for some cause or other: "Peace in Vietnam" or "Legalise Drugs" or some such dream that money could not buy. We all got very stoned with him in his backstage dressing room before he went on. He played like an angel on all the dust on planet Venus. After a while, he took a solo and his notes started soaring, weaving acoustic gordian knots inside every one of the 35,000 (full house) brains that were riveted to his nuclear powered guitar, making each one of our skulls feel like the inside of Chartres Cathedral on Judgement Day. He took off, soaring higher and higher across the uncharted musical stratospheres of sound where no composer has ever trodden, not even Stockhausen or Cage. And there he cruised and glided, dove and reascended in patterns of spirals and arabesques masterminded by epileptic spiders, dragonflies and plumed serpents fornicating phoenixes on fire ... when suddenly he stopped; maybe he got scared by the vastness of his own inner space, I don't know, but he stopped and waited for a reaction ... The entire audience of the Garden held their breath in awe. Not a single person dared to pollute the divine silence with the vulgar clapping of hands.

This he did not understand. He threw his guitar on to the floor of the stage and fired a few angry (or anguished) words into the microphone, "We don't seem to understand each other tonight!" and floated off the stage, disappearing from our lives. He was so afraid to lose his audience that he thought he lost it when, on the contrary, he had them riveted to his notes, to his new dimensions ... From then on he just played the blues and died a few months later.

Mati Klarwein - January 1995
Deya, Mallorca

This poster by Martin Sharp uses a Linda McCartney shot as its base image, taken when the Jimi Hendrix Experience opened for the Young Rascals in New York's Central Park on July 5, 1967. The reputation of this Australian designer was established with his work for the group Cream. This poster also appeared on one of the covers of Britain's *OZ* magazine, the controversial standard-bearer for the UK's underground press; and on the cover of *Get Down: A Decade Of Rock Posters*, compiled and written by the pioneering British underground writer Mick Farren.

1967: Exploding Guitar. Martin Sharp.

1967: Exploding Guitar. Martin Sharp.

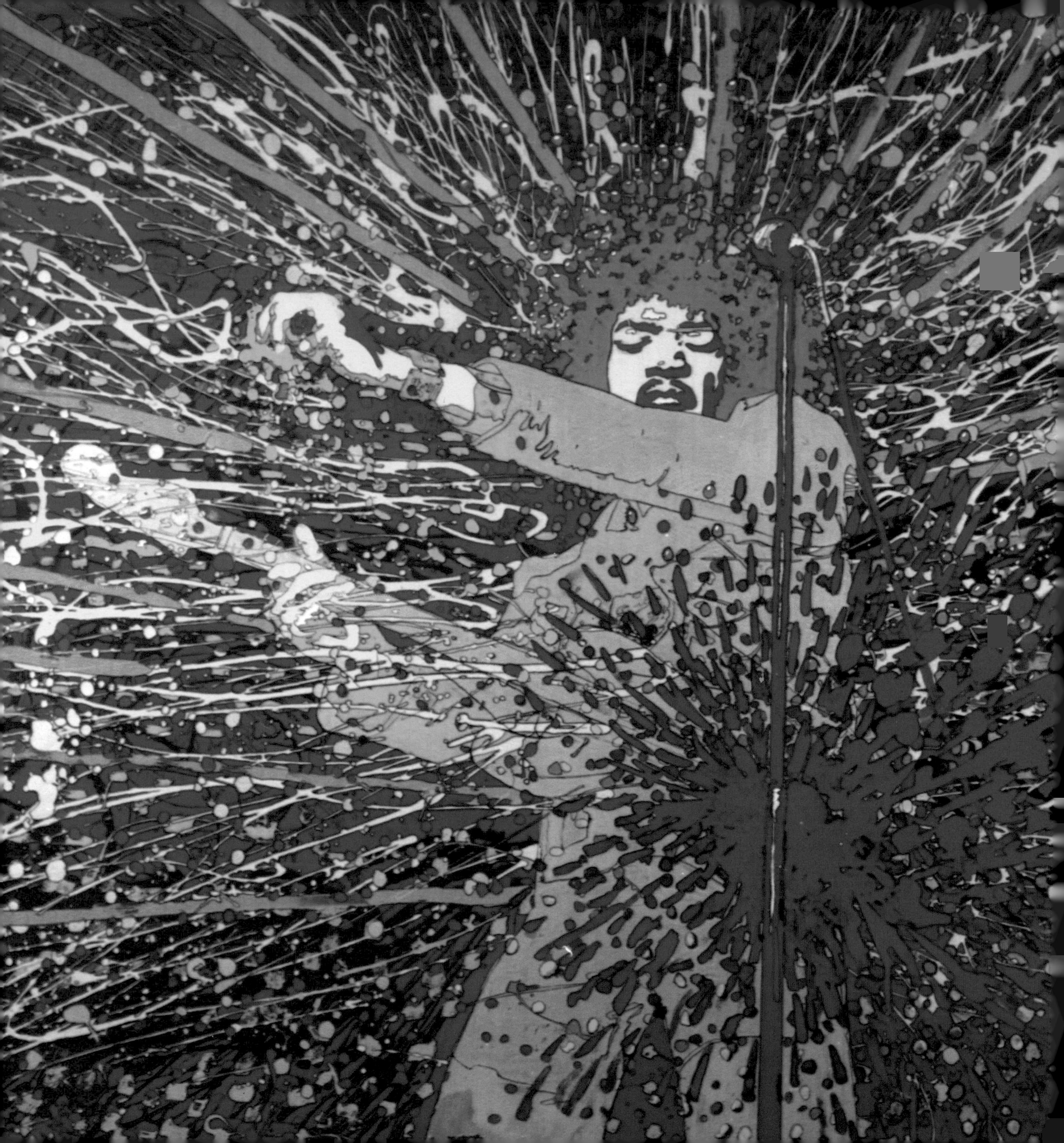

CAUGHT LIKE A BRIGHT BIRD

The first time I ever saw him was, after all, like the last. He was trapped by a huge dooby crowd on a high stage in the corner of a cattle shed in Spalding. The air was hot and rank because all the sliding cattle doors were shut but one and there were no windows. As usual, an unlimited number of tickets had been sold and the promoters had split, leaving the kids to struggle in the heat and the dirt while the police snooped around them with dogs trained to sniff out the drugs that none of them had the money to buy.

We got in, in the chaos, for nothing, and there was Jimi caught like a bright bird underneath a corrugated-iron roof in the stink of the cattle shit and sweating English youth. The crowd was so dense that those who fainted couldn't even fall down. Jimi was wrestling to get his guitar in tune and cursing the Orange gear that they had to use, as crappy then as now. The kids were restive and abusive. Jimi began to play and the sound was terrible so he stopped. They jeered so he stepped downstage and yelled, "Fuck you. I'm gonna get this guitar in tune if it takes me all night." Then, as now, they didn't care whether "Hey Joe" was in tune or not, they just wanted to hear noise and adulate. They wanted him to give head to the guitar and rub it over his cock. They didn't want to hear him play, but Jimi wanted, as he always wanted, to play sweet and high. So he did it, and he fucked with his guitar, and they moaned and swayed about, and he looked at them heavily and knew that they couldn't hear what he was trying to do and they never would.

Germaine Greer, extracted from Hey, Jimi, where you gonna run to now? OZ, October 1970.

Hey Joe

Hey Joe

I'm goin' down to shoot my old lady,
You know I caught her messin' round with another man
Shot her one more time again, baby!
I'm goin' way down south,
Way down to Mexico way!

Photograph : Ivan Oliver

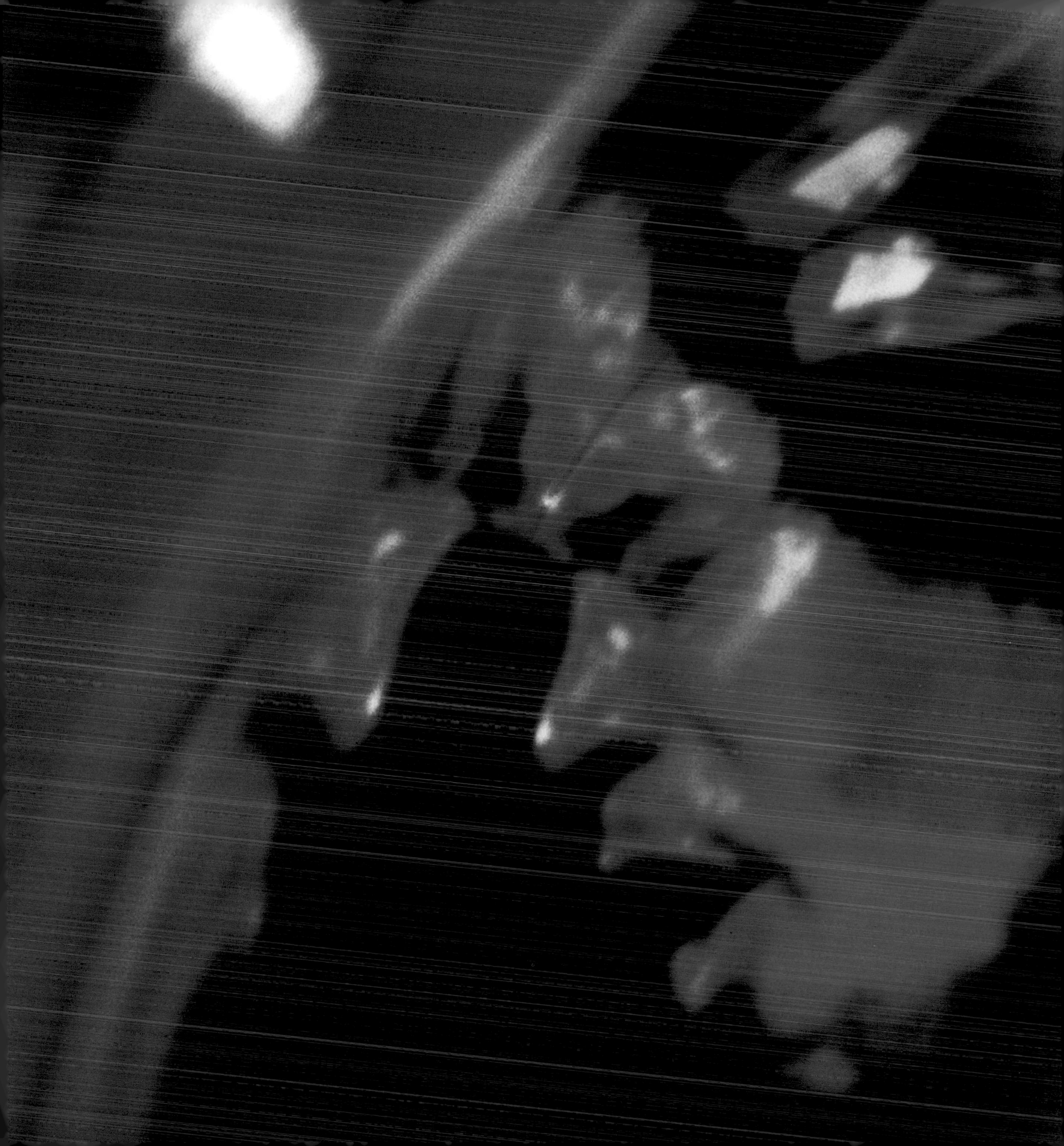

1983: A MERMAN I SHOULD TURN TO BE

Gypsy Boy sits shivering in the bar of the abandoned motel by the shore, waiting for Nightbird, obsessively picking at his unamplified guitar as if it were a scab, burning the midnight lamp. The power lines had been down for over a week, and the oil-fired generator in the shed out back functioned only intermittently, so most of the time he was dependent for light on torches powered by batteries scavenged from the gift shop, and for heat on odd items of busted furniture which he burned on what used to be the stage. Sometimes he was careful not to risk torching the entire building; sometimes, after a few drinks from the bar's remaining bottles, he didn't care whether he burned it down or not. So far, he hadn't.

Later, when he attempted to recollect the time he spent there, it seemed to have lasted little longer than a single night: a sweaty, hallucinatory, toss-and-turn, damp-pillowed fever-dream of a night, but a single night nevertheless. At the time, though, it felt as though he'd never been anywhere else, and never would be anywhere else.

Two nights before the war finally broke out, Gypsy Boy came to the Cherokee Inn, soaking wet from the blizzard raging outside. He'd hitch-hiked from the Greyhound station carrying only a Stratocaster with one spare set of strings, a Twin Reverb amp with a loose output valve and a couple of missing control knobs, just under three hundred dollars in limp, torn bills, and a single suitcase stuffed with crumpled, sweat-stained stage clothes and scraps of paper covered with illegible scrawlings which he claimed were poems and song lyrics. He checked into the cheapest room they had, telling the bored Puerto Rican boy behind the reception desk that if a Miss Bird arrived or called, he wanted to know immediately, day or night, but that if a Miss Dagger enquired after him they must under no circumstances admit that he was there, or even that they'd ever heard of him. The boy yawned, scribbled something next to his name on the register, and handed him his key. He hauled his suitcase, amplifier and guitar across the courtyard, past the filthy swimming pool, let himself into his room. He surveyed the stained wallpaper, the threadbare blankets, the worn-out TV, the flyblown mirror, the cracked toilet seat, and the dusty bath. The tubercular grinding of the heater just about masked the pounding rain and the howling wind battering the walls of the room, but it couldn't drown out the sounds of the couple fighting next door. He crawled between the sheets and eventually drifted into a troubled sleep which was only fractionally more restful than no sleep at all.

Nightbird didn't call. Conserving his money, Gypsy Boy haunted the motel like some disconsolate ghost with post-adolescent acne and a raggedy, half-grown-out process. Occasionally he'd appear in the coffee shop, pushing the watery scrambled eggs around his plate and nursing the same cup of coffee for hours on end, but most of the time, he stayed in his room, watching TV, following the news around the dial, hearing the President attempting, over and over, to reassure the country that the war would easily be won, no matter what kind of weapons the enemy were using. The occasional Cassandras who warned that the use of dirty weapons, anywhere in the world, would eventually render the entire planetary surface uninhabitable were mocked both by official spokesmen and by the smiling, self-assured anchors. The Cassandras insisted that it

So my darling and I, Make love in the sand, Last moment ever on dry land

didn't matter who was fighting or where, but what they were fighting with. The anchors smiled, the President reassured, the networks cut to commercials whenever a Cassandra looked like he or she was about to win the argument.

Once, towards the end of the second week, Gypsy Boy attempted to spin out his decreasing funds by sitting in with the band who played Thursday, Friday and Saturday nights in the bar, but after the first set they told him he played too loud and sounded too weird and was scaring the customers, all seven of them. As he lugged his guitar and amplifier back to his room, he thought he heard the sax player mutter something about goddam crazy niggers and the rest of the band, huddled round a table near the stage with their cigarettes and beers and shots of Black Jack, erupted into cawing laughter which he fancied he could still hear even when he was back in his room, sprawled out on his bed watching Huntley and Brinkley. The worn-out picture tube enveloped them in fuzzy, garish reds and blues which blended, when the winds jarred the aerial, into a sickly mauve halo.

Sometimes, he would reread the tattered comic book he'd found in the coffee shop one morning after breakfast. It was issue 352 of Astro Man, one of his childhood favourites, and in the lead story, Astro Man, patrolling a distant sector of the galaxy, landed on an idyllic planet populated by gentle, peaceful people living a pastoral tribal lifestyle, kind of like Native Americans. Astro Man fell in love with a beautiful maiden there, and promised to return on his next swing through that sector, but on his next stop, he became ensnared by a seductive sorceress who almost succeeded in trapping him in her world forever. After his escape, he returned to the Indian planet, but found it devastated by nuclear war, and the remains of its formerly peaceful people fighting over the ruins. Apparently time moved much faster there, the few weeks he'd been away had been the equivalent of a thousand of their years, and the girl he loved was long dead. The comic-book company had hired some new artists since the last time he'd read Astro Man, and all the characters looked different. Now Astro Man looked a little like him, the lovely tribal maiden like Nightbird, and the evil sorceress like Dolly. He read the story over and over to distract himself from the news, but somehow it failed to cheer him up. Nightbird still didn't call, but then neither did Dolly.

By the beginning of his third week, Gypsy Boy was out of money. He'd tried to save money by only eating once a day and allowing himself only three cigarettes a day and a couple of beers each weekend, but eventually he'd had to go to the desk and confess to the Puerto Rican boy that he was broke. The boy had sucked his teeth contemptuously and gone to get the manager, a doughy woman in a stained overall, with brassy bottle-blonde hair and eyes like pale-blue marbles. In the end they cut a deal: he handed over his amp and in exchange was allowed to keep the room for another five days.

By now, the tone of the war news had shifted. The President wasn't quite so reassuring, the anchors' smiles weren't quite so self-assured, and the Cassandras were getting a rather more respectful hearing. The winds were steadily increasing in strength, and a cloud of death was blowing from the war zone towards the coast.

Photograph : David Magnus / Rex Features

The word "evacuation" began to be heard more and more frequently, and it was suggested that the President had a master plan to save the population, though no one was prepared to state exactly what that plan might be. A friendly chambermaid who occasionally sneaked him a hamburger or a pack of cigarettes told him that her brother was in the military and was claiming that a fleet of giant space shuttles was going to fly millions of people to safety under an airtight dome on Mars. A tabloid newspaper suggested that the answer was an undersea colony capable of sheltering Americans until the planet was habitable again, fit for them to inherit. However, since the same paper also claimed that the President was having a passionate affair with the movies' favourite blonde, Gypsy Boy didn't take that one too seriously.

At the end of the week, he still hadn't heard from Nightbird. He went back to the desk, gave the doughy woman his guitar, returned to the room and reread the Astro Man *book, dividing his attention between the garish four-colour figures on the page and the mauve blurs on the TV screen. They were talking evacuation again, this time within the next forty-eight hours. Apparently the tabloid had been right after all: huge submarines were already massing offshore to take the population down to their new home on the ocean floor.*

Everybody packed up and moved out, including the doughy woman, the chambermaid, and the Puerto Rican. Gypsy Boy decided to stay. With a sidelong grin, the doughy woman flipped him the master keys to the Cherokee Inn. The first thing he did was to retrieve his guitar and amp from under her desk in the back office, haul them down to the bar, and plug in. The red light on the amp's front panel glowed reassuringly at him, the loose output valve buzzed and hummed. He kicked in the front of the cigarette machine, retrieved a pack of Marlboros, lit up, turned everything up to ten, and wailed till his fingers bled. He fell asleep sitting on the stage, the amp still humming to him throughout the long, stormy night. When he awoke, the power had gone, and the phones were dead.

Exploring the motel's storage rooms, he found torches, lanterns, and a freezer full of gently defrosting hamburgers and eggs. In the back yard, a derelict shed contained an ancient generator which, with much cursing and a couple of ripped fingernails, he managed to start up. He left the amp permanently switched on so that its hum and its red light would tell him whether the electricity was flowing or not. Occasionally he went outside, but the air was growing steadily fouler, and he felt sick and weak when he breathed it.

The woman found him curled up on the stage, his guitar clasped in his arms, huddling for warmth next to the embers of a small fire he'd built from the last bar stool. She shook him gently by the shoulder. As he awoke, his gummy eyes at first refusing to focus, she appeared to him, wreathed in the mauve haze he remembered from the TV set in his old room. He seemed to see two shifting figures, sometimes standing side by side, sometimes blurring into one. The woman on the left was tall, African-featured, with broad shoulders and heavy breasts; the one on the right was small, lithe, impish, Cherokee.

He hauled himself up on one elbow, rubbed his eyes, stared up at Dolly and Nightbird as they smiled down at him. His eyes finally settled into focus, and now there was but one woman, with Dolly's height and strength and Nightbird's elfin smile and liquid grace. The halo still surrounded her, but it was no longer the sickly hue he had seen on the TV screen. Instead, it was now a healing purple aura of boundless depth, richness and compassion. She helped him gently to his feet and held him close. As her purple aura enveloped him, the air was chilly and foul no more; now it was warm and fresh and sweet. He felt strength returning to his limbs, and a new clarity augmenting his vision. Even his hearing was different: the world seemed to vibrate harmoniously, and in the distance he could hear one huge, all-encompassing chord, in which every note he could imagine, and a few of which he could never even have dreamed, happily co-existed. With that part of his mind which was still Gypsy Boy, he reflected that he had never quite understood what "harmony" was before that moment.

Protected by the purple glow, Astro Man and the Angel flew towards the shore without even a single glance back at the ruins of the Cherokee Inn. They plunged into the ocean and dived down, past the fleet of submarines, past the huge plastic domes which bubbled the ocean floor. Not a single drop of water touched their bodies as they hurtled along the coast. Slowing to a comfortable drift, they rolled over and over until they could see, reaching down to them through the swelling murky waters, what appeared to be the first rays of a new rising sun.

New York drowned as they held hands.

(For J.G. Ballard and Michael Moorcock)
Charles Shaar Murray

Art : Joel Axelrad / iQ Videographics / Retna

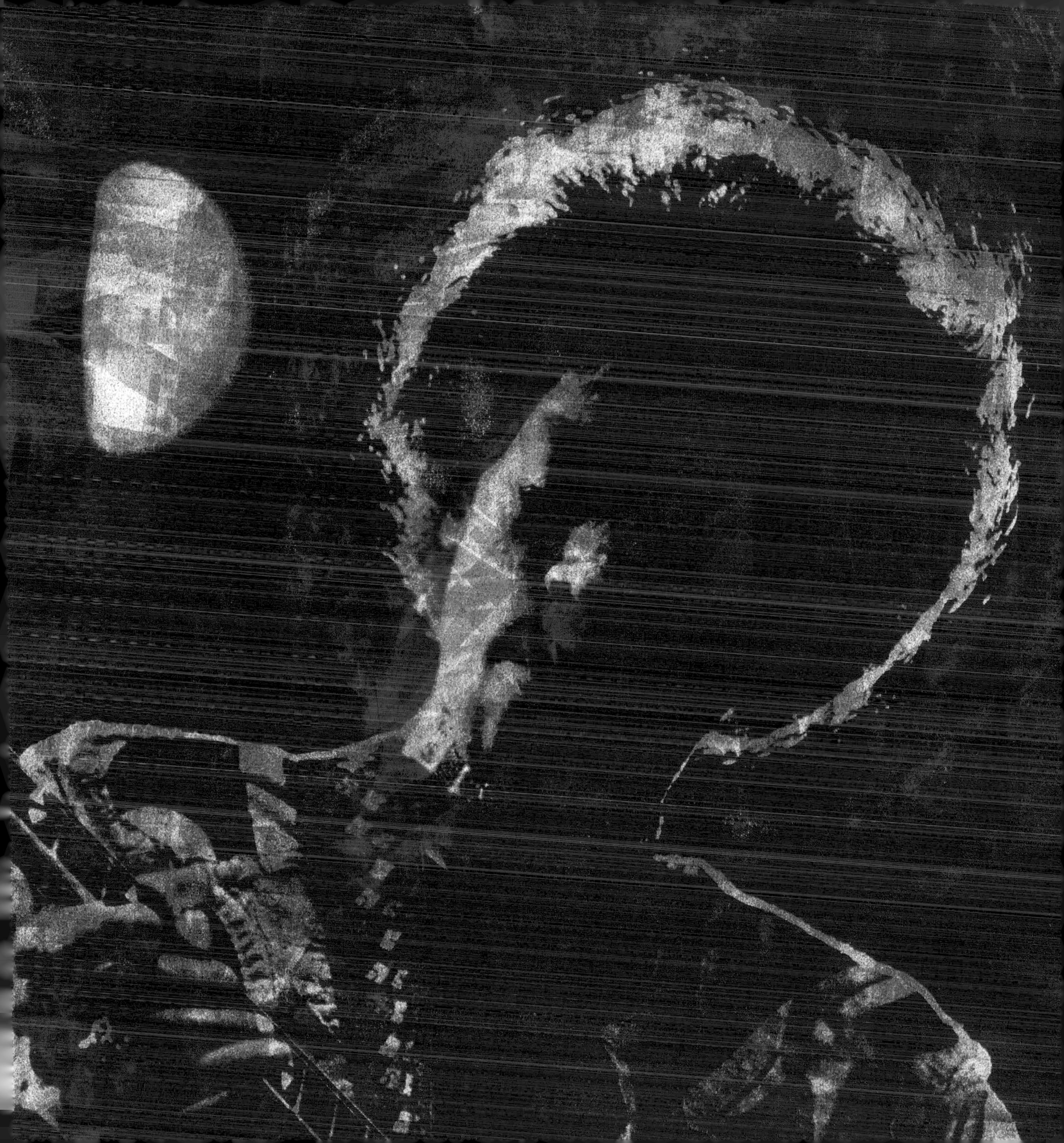

it's Dead it's a Ghost now

Think about tomorrow not yesterday

Think about tomorrow not yesterday

"I'm not sure how I feel about the Experience now.
I died a thousand times in that group and was born again.
But after a while you have to get yourself straightened out...

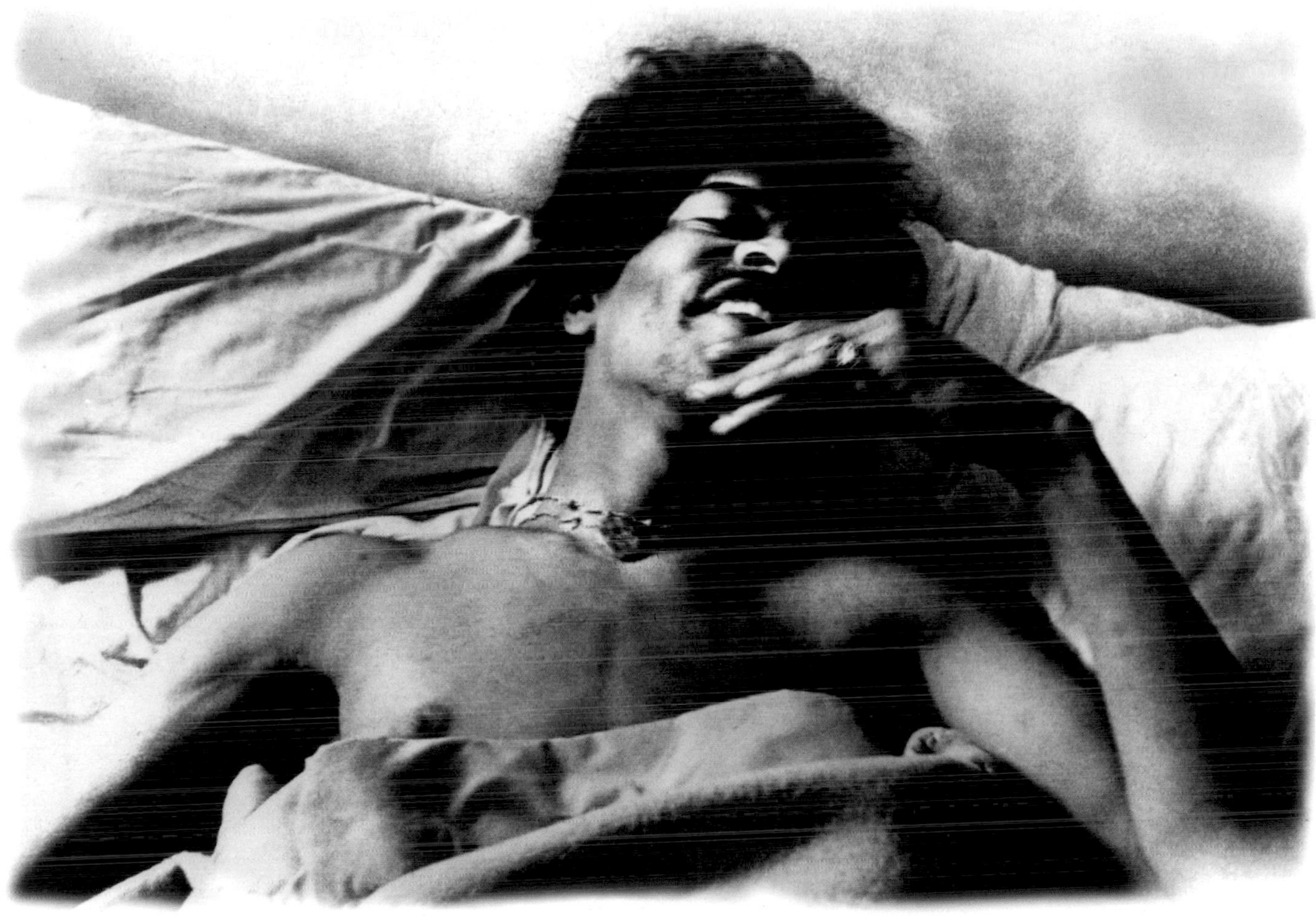

it's a ghost now - it's dead, like back pages in a diary.
I'm into new things and I want to think about tomorrow, not yesterday."

Photograph : Roz Kelly / Michael Ochs Archives

Trumpets and violins I can hear in the distance,
I think they're callin' our name.

(Are You Experienced?)

Photograph : Michael Ochs Archives

I used to see the numbers one-nine-six-six in my dreams. I had very strange feelings that I was here for something and I was going to get a chance to be heard. I got the guitar together because that was all I had.

Music is going to break the way because music is in a spiritual thing of its own. It's like the waves of the ocean. You can't just cut out the perfect wave and take it home with you.

A musician, if he's a messenger, is like a child who hasn't been handled too many times by man, hasn't had too many fingerprints across his brain. That's why music is so much heavier than anything you ever felt.

It's more than music. It's like church, like a foundation for the lost or potentially lost...We're making our music into a new kind of Bible, a Bible you can carry in your hearts, one that will give a physical feeling.

When it was time for us to play on stage I was all shaky, so I had to play behind the curtains. I just couldn't get up in front. And then you get so very discouraged. You hear different bands playing around you and the guitar player always seems like he's so much better than you are. Most people give up at this point, but it's best not to. Just keep on, just keep on. Sometimes you are going to be so frustrated you'll hate the guitar, but all of this is just a part of learning. If you stick with it you're going to be rewarded. If you're very stubborn you can make it.

We play very, very loud. We play loud to create a certain effect, to make it all as physical as possible.

The world revolves around sex. Music should be matched with human emotions and if you can tell me a more human one than sex, then you've got me fooled.

Photograph : Gered Mankowitz

ANYBODY!

When I was staying in Harlem my hair was really long, like sometimes I might tie it up or do something with it. I'd be walking down the street and all of a sudden the cats, or girls, old ladies - ANYBODY! - there just peekin' out, sayin', "Ough, what's this supposed to be, Black Jesus?" or "What is this, the circus or something?" God! Even in your own section. Your own people hurt you more.

Purple And Gold (1992)

From black and white originals, shot by Gered Mankowitz at his Mason's Yard studio in March 1967.

"How is it in London anyway? This pop business is so much harder than people think. It's nerve-racking and mind-bending. The people who dig ditches for a living don't know how lucky they are."

My Red is so
confident
He flashes trophies of war
and ribbons of euphoria
Orange is young, full of
daring
But very unsteady for
the first go round
My yellow in this case is
not so mellow
In fact, I'm trying to say that
it's frightened like me

Photograph / Art : Gered Mankowitz / David Costa

Photograph : Rancurel / Lampard

From The Experience's fourth ever date. They played three French provincial shows with local megastar Johnny Hallyday before closing this mini-tour at the Paris Olympia on October 18 1966. Also included on the last night's bill was The Brian Auger Trinity, whose organist Brian Auger, bass-player Dave Ambrose and singer Julie Driscoll are also pictured.

JIMI BY MILES DAVIS

I first met Jimi when his manager called up and wanted me to introduce him to the way I was playing and putting my music together. Jimi liked what I had done on Kind Of Blue and some other stuff and wanted to add more jazz elements to what he was doing. He liked the way Coltrane played with all those other sheets of sound, and he played the guitar in a similar way. Plus, he said that he had heard the guitar voicing that I used in the way I played the trumpet. So we started getting together...

He was a real nice guy, quiet but intense, and was nothing like people thought he was. He was just the opposite of the wild and crazy image he presented on the stage. When we started getting together and talking about music, I found out that he couldn't read music. Betty (Mabry) had a party for him sometime in 1969 at my house on West 77th. I couldn't be there because I had to be in the studio that night recording, so I left some music for him to read and then we'd talk about it later. (Some people wrote some shit that I didn't come to the party for him because I didn't like having a party for a man in my house. That's a lot of bullshit.)

When I called back home from the studio to speak to Jimi about the music I had left him, I found out he didn't read music. There are a lot of great musicians who don't read music – black and white – that I have known and respected and played with. So I didn't think less of Jimi because of that. Jimi was just a great, natural musician – self-taught. He would pick up things from whoever he was around, and he picked up things quick. Once he heard it he really had it down. We would be talking, and I would be telling him technical shit like, "Jimi, you know, when you play the diminished chord . . . ." I would see this lost look come into his face and I would say, "Okay, okay, I forgot." I would just play it for him on the piano or on the horn, and he would get it faster than a motherfucker. He had a natural ear for hearing music. So I'd play different shit for him, show him that way. Or I'd play him a record of mine or Trane's and explain to him what we were doing. Then he started incorporating things I told him into his albums. It was great. He influenced me, and I influenced him, and that's the way great music is always made. Everybody showing everybody else something and then moving on from there.

But Jimi was also close to hillbilly, country music played by them mountain white people. That's why he had those two English guys in his band, because a lot of white English musicians liked that American hillbilly music. The best he sounded to me was when he had Buddy Miles on drums and Billy Cox on bass. Jimi was playing that Indian kind of shit, or he'd play those funny little melodies he doubled up on his guitar. I loved it when he doubled up shit like that. He used to play 6/8 all the time when he was with them white English guys and that's what made him sound like a hillbilly to me. Just that concept he was doing with that. But when he started playing with Buddy and Billy in the Band Of Gypsys, I think he brought what he was doing all the way out. But the record companies and white people liked him better when he had the white guys in his band, just like a lot of white people like to talk about me when I was doing the nonet thing – the Birth Of The Cool thing, or when I did those other albums with Gil Evans or Bill Evans because they always like to see white people up in black shit, so that they can say they had something to do with it. But Jimi Hendrix came from the blues, like me. We understood each other right away because of that. He was a great blues guitarist.

Michael Ochs Archives

Drugs are, in general, a very hip and mysterious experience.
I just used them for a certain thing, as a step towards seeing it both ways, if you like.
All Indians have different ways of stimulation - their own steps towards God, spiritual forms,
or whatever....The soul must rule, not drugs.
You should rule yourself and give God a chance.

Drugs are, in general, a very hip and mysterious experience.
I just used them for a certain thing, as a step towards seeing it both ways, if you like.
All Indians have different ways of stimulation - their own steps towards God, spiritual forms,
or whatever....The soul must rule, not drugs.
You should rule yourself and give God a chance.

Drugs are, in general, a very hip and mysterious experience.
I just used them for a certain thing, as a step towards seeing it both ways, if you like.
All Indians have different ways of stimulation - their own steps towards God, spiritual forms,
or whatever....The soul must rule, not drugs.
You should rule yourself and give God a chance.

Photograph : Jean-Noel Coghe
Art : Moebius

Photograph : Ira Cohen

"Looking at your photographs is like looking through butterfly wings."

Jimi's dislike of having the camera pointed straight at him captured vividly during a February shoot at Ira Cohen's attic studio in New York. The distortion was caused by Cohen photographing Jimi's reflection in silver foil.

Cherokee

"I hear music in my head all the time. Sometimes it makes my brain throb and the room starts to turn. I feel I'm going mad. With this music we will paint pictures of earth and space so that the listener can be taken somewhere. It's going to be something that will open up a new sense in people's minds."

CHEROKEE : Bruno Tilley (1992)

I tell you, when I die I'm going to have a jam session. I want people to go wild and freak out. And knowing me, I'll probably get busted at my own funeral. I shall have them playing everything I did musically, everything I enjoyed doing most. The music will be played loud and it will be our music. I won't have any Beatles songs, but I'll have a few of Eddie Cochran's things and a whole lot of blues. Roland Kirk will be there and I'll try and get Miles Davis along if he feels like making it. For that it's almost worth dying. Just for the funeral.

Crash Landing

1975 : The Art that was used for the cover of the posthumously released album, Crash Landing.

A1.Albert King. A2.BB King. A3.Chuck Berry. A4.Hubert Sumlin. A5.Lightning Slim. A6.Buddy Guy. B1.Howlin' Wolf. B2.John Lee Hooker. B3.Curtis Mayfield. B4.Lowell Fulson. B5.Little Walter. B6.Johnny Jenkins. C1.Robert Johnson. C2.Muddy Waters. C3.Albert Collins. C4.Earl Hooker. C5.Johnny 'Guitar' Watson. C6.Willie Dixon. D1.Jimmy Reed. D2.Young Buddy Guy. D3.T-Bone Walker. D4.Ike Turner. D5.Lightning Hopkins. D6.Earl King. E1.Freddie King. E2.Robert Jnr Lockwood. E3.Sonny Boy Williamson. E4.Lonnie Johnson. E5.Pee Wee Crayton. E6.Little Walter. F1.Clarence 'Gatemouth' Brown. F2.Son House. F3.Guitar Slim. F4.Elmore James. F5.Otis Rush. F6.Young BB King.

Blues (1994) : Richard Bull for Stylorouge & Alan Douglas.

Commissioned for the cover of the 1994 release Blues and based on a theme used in "Cherokee" by Bruno Tilley. Produced completely digitally with a view to simulate multiple screenprinting.

I wish they'd had electric guitars in cotton fields back in the good old days. A whole lot of things would've been straightened out.

If the cards were down in reality I would have to admit, even then, that what I was doing was just nowhere with what he was doing.
ERIC CLAPTON

Hendrix was one of those guys that was so explosive, him and John Coltrane - way ahead of their time. Jimi basically played the blues but he added to it.
BUDDY GUY

He played his own shit, he didn't play nobody else's stuff like what they do now. Jimi was original.
ALBERT COLLINS

What people had been used to was kind of dressed up, watered down soul music. But for someone like Jimi to come along was so powerful. As is the way with musicians, we just sort of dug up all our heroes and compared them and we actually thought the same. He liked Freddie and BB King, Robert Johnson and Buddy Guy. We liked all the same people. I mean, it was such a thrill because it was all second hand for me, it was something I learned from records. This guy had been among them and was one of them.....
ERIC CLAPTON

Courtesy : AYEI

Waterfall, nothing can harm me at all.
Some people say daydreaming's for all the, huh! lazy-minded fools with nothin' else to do. So let them laugh, laugh at me.

(May This Be Love)

White collar conservative flashin' down the street
Pointin' their plastic finger at me.
They're hopin' that soon my kind will drop and die
But I'm gonna wave my free flag high

(If 6 was 9)

Jealousy, envy, waits behind him,
her fiery green gown sneers at the grassy ground
Blue are the life-giving waters taken for granted,
They quietly understand
Once happy turquoise armies lay opposite ready,
But wonder why the fight is on.

(Bold As Love)

Third Stone From The Sun
The Birth Chart Of Jimi Hendrix

by Laura Boomer & Neil Spencer

James Marshall Hendrix, nee Johnny Alan Hendrix
b. 10.15 a.m. November 27, 1942, Seattle Washington
d. 11.25 a.m. September 18, 1970, London England

"The night I was born, the moon turned a fire red." – Voodoo Child

Throughout his short life, Jimi Hendrix maintained that he was not from this planet at all. He was, he said, a 'visitor', a traveller, a cosmic gypsy. He assigned various locations to his origins; an asteroid belt off the coast of Mars, the planet Jupiter, or simply the nebulous regions of the astral planes, which he claimed he had visited as a boy.

Wherever he came from, when Jimi Hendrix touched down on planet earth, the Sun and Moon stood respectively in the eastern and western sky. All but two of the planets were above the horizon. In the east, the twenty-fourth degree of the constellation of Sagittarius was rising over the horizon, with the centaur's arrows pointing directly to the core of our galaxy.

Hendrix's birth chart clearly illustrates the recurring themes of his life and work. Johnny Alan the abandoned child; James Marshall the schoolboy outsider; Jimmy the aspiring teenage musician; Paratrooper Hendrix; Jimi the guitar wizard; the hippie icon; the compulsive but unhappy lover; the drug casualty and even the posthumous legend. All are facets of the man that can be read in the astrological configuration of planets, star signs and 'houses'.

All the planets in Jimi's chart fall in fire, air or water signs – he conspicuously lacks earth's practicality. In particular his excess of elemental fire (through Sagittarius and Leo) points to Jimi's wild, volatile tendencies.

The 'bowl' shape described by Jimi's planets, with all but two falling in the upper half of the chart, represents a receptive, self-contained individual who receives knowledge and emotional understanding through his experiences. Others then 'dip' into and learn from him.

That the majority of planets are in the sky, above the self-relationship axis symbolised by the horizon, indicates that an outgoing character like Hendrix enjoyed very little privacy, as though he were constantly on show.

The chart overall shows a loving, warm-hearted individual, highly spirited and open to divine inspiration. The chart also reflects Jimi's deep enchantment with the primal elements. Images of arcing skies, consuming fires and majestic oceans litter Jimi's songs in a way that is still unparalleled in popular music; themes we can examine in more detail as we go through the chart.

Central Image : Lucia Solazzi / John O'Brian

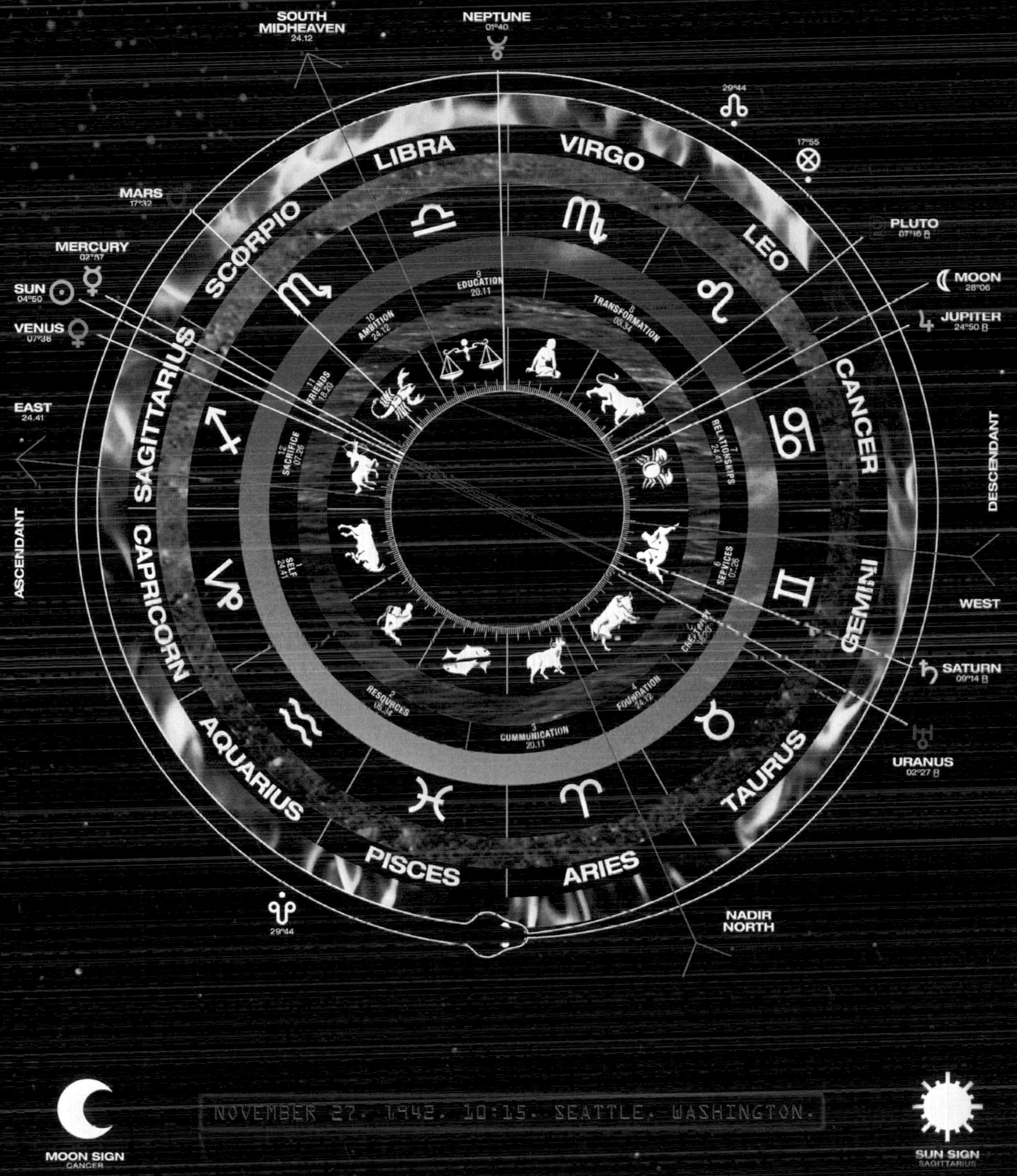

SOUTH MIDHEAVEN
24.12

NEPTUNE
01°40

29°44

17°55

MARS
17°32

MERCURY
02°57

SUN
04°50

VENUS
07°38

EAST
24.41

ASCENDANT

PLUTO
07°16 ℞

MOON
28°06

JUPITER
24°50 ℞

DESCENDANT

WEST

SATURN
09°14 ℞

URANUS
02°27 ℞

NADIR
NORTH

29°44

LIBRA

VIRGO

SCORPIO

LEO

SAGITTARIUS

CANCER

CAPRICORN

GEMINI

AQUARIUS

TAURUS

PISCES

ARIES

9
EDUCATION
20.11

10
AMBITION
24.12

8
TRANSFORMATION
05.34

11
FRIENDS
18.20

7
RELATIONSHIPS
24.41

12
SACRIFICE
07.26

1
SELF
24.41

6
SERVICES
07.26

2
RESOURCES
05.34

4
FOUNDATION
24.12

3
COMMUNICATION
20.11

MOON SIGN
CANCER

SUN SIGN
SAGITTARIUS

Sagittarius: Highway Chile

Jimi's Sun in Sagittarius is joined by Mercury and Venus, while his all important ascendant is likewise the Archer. The arrow-shooting centaur symbolises human need to overcome animal instinct with intellectual agility, to discover the higher truths available to us.

The Sagittarian impetus is to extract the most out of every experience – "I want to see and hear everything" as Jimi sang – and with the aptly named Experience Jimi had the opportunity to deal with many of Sagittarius's bigger issues: travel, philosophy, and religion.

Typically, Sagittarian artists engage with 'the big picture', with the laws of the cosmos. William Blake's intricate cosmologies and John Milton's epic Paradise Lost *are typical of Sagittarian visionaries. Hendrix's art likewise conjures up sweeping landscapes and logic-defying voyages across time and space.*

Jimi's Sagittarian impulses were hugely magnified by the fact that in addition to the Sun – the inner spirit, the life path – the personal planets of Mercury (intellect, mind, communicator) and Venus (lover, sense of self-worth) and his ascendant were also Sagittarian. Jimi's sense of adventure was therefore colossal, but the twelfth house position of this Sagittarian 'band of gypsies' meant that his voyages of discovery were often illusory. Ultimately, Jimi's Sagittarian quest was driven by, in the words of his biographer Harry Shapiro, "a firm belief that he had a divine message to impart, that it was his duty to bring a vision of love and healing to the world".

Sagittarius Ascending: Are You Experienced?

The ascendant indicates appearance, how one comes across to others, the persona. A Sagittarius ascendant is typically a flamboyant character who mentally or physically towers over others. Sagittarius ascendant is the sign of the wisdom seeker looking for a philosophy to place their profound questions into perspective. Once answers are found, their impetus is to tell them to the rest of the world – Sagittarians are renowned for letting others know what they believe, including some tactless home truths.

Jimi's chart ruler, the planet which governs his ascendant sign, is Jupiter, the 'sky father', the largest planet in our solar system. Jupiter's colour is purple, a hue which crops up repeatedly in Hendrix's lyrics. As the King of the Gods, Jupiter brings

joy, and exudes the kind of jovial optimism that Jimi communicated on and offstage.

What is often strange about Sagittarius ascending is the rapid shift from wisdom-seeker to clown prince, from smart to silly. When either too relaxed or too fired-up (as only those with the hedonistic and fiery Jupiter ruling the chart can be), they begin to masquerade a clumsy animal instinct, a love of 'goofing off'.

From the ascendant one moves anti-clockwise around the chart quickly in the first instance because there is no planetary action in the first five houses of the chart.

Uranus Conjunct Saturn: Stone Free

The set of planetary dynamics represented by the Uranus-Saturn conjunction belongs to everyone born around 1941'42. This was the moment when Uranus, the planet of altruistic ideals, latched onto the earthy 'Time Lord' Saturn in the communicative sign of Gemini.

Uranian energy is unpredictable and disruptive, while the patriarchal Saturn represents tradition, continuity and preservation. It's an explosive combination. Jimi's generation felt compelled to break obsolete rules, even though they knew they would continually run up against authority. Freedom of the spirit was his generation's key to cultural and intellectual development.

In Jimi's case, this sigil falls in the sixth house, which concerns duty and service to others. For Jimi, challenging the 'white collar plastic conservatives' was an act of conscience, an unrefusable call to duty.

The Uranus-Saturn dynamic also manifested in Jimi's playing. He paid full honour to the enduring traditions of the blues (Saturn), while adding to them the explosive power chords and feedback of electrically charged Uranus.

The Eighth House: Lord knows I'm a Voodoo Chile

Moving up to the eighth house, the house of hidden, occult knowledge, we encounter Jimi's chart ruler Jupiter, an emotional Cancer Moon and Pluto, the 'Lord of the Underworld', in wide conjunction. It's a combination of awesome potency. Jimi's celebrated sexual magnetism, his intuitive feel for occult matters, and his extra-sensory insights are all to be found here. The magic of telepathic contact and otherworldly phenomena became, for Jimi, almost routine.

Aliens

Jimi visited by the long arm of the law backstage at The Civic Auditorium, Bakersfield in California on October 26th, the day after the group's third album - Electric Ladyland - was released.

Photograph : Ron Rafaelli / Michael Ochs Archives

(1968)

Jupiter doubles the intensity of any planet it touches, and Jupiter in the nurturing sign of Cancer is considered 'exalted', its best placing in the zodiac. The presence of both the Moon and Jimi's chart-ruler Jupiter in the aquatic sign of Cancer points to his abiding obsessions with the ocean. Born and raised by the sea, Jimi was haunted by water – by rain, by waterfalls, and by the power and mystery of the ocean depths, the source of all life.

Oceanic imagery figures powerfully in Jimi's work. In "Are You Experienced" Jimi promises us we will "watch the sun rise from the bottom of the sea". In "Angel", he sings of "the sweet love between the moon and the deep blue sea". Above all, he fantasises of becoming a merman in a drowned world in "1983, A Merman I Should Turn To Be", an image fashioned from Jupiter in Cancer.

Jupiter in the eighth indicates legacies and longevity, but the Moon, sandwiched between Jupiter and Pluto, the omnipotent ruler of life and death, also represents Jimi's posthumous status.

Moon In Cancer in The Eighth: Moon, Turn the tides … gently, gently away.

Behind Hendrix's public bravura lay an intensely shy man, his lunar feelings locked within the safety of the Cancer crab shell. Friends and acquaintances all attest to Jimi's shyness and reticence.

The moon in its own sign of Cancer brings other qualities: intuition, imagination, and depth of feeling. But Cancer moon's propensity for addictions and cravings is also intensified by Jupiter, making it nigh on impossible for Hendrix to let go of any emotional crutch, even when his habit was downright evil. Moon in Cancer also gives violent mood swings – Jimi's 'Manic Depression' – which can't have been helped by the come-downs from his copious drug intake.

Apart from being the chart's emotional anchor, the Moon also indicates a person's home, and their relationship with their mother. Jimi's Moon in Cancer indicates an intense involvement with his mother, Lucille, despite her physical absence. Lucille's consumptive health, her abandonment of Jimi, her self-destructive urges, and her early death when Jimi was 15 are all consistent with the moon's conjunction to Pluto in the Scorpionic 'House of Death'.

From beyond the grave, the dark figure of Lucille continued to haunt Jimi's psyche. Several of his best songs, among them "Gypsy Eyes", and "Angel", concern her, while in "Belly button Window", Jimi wonders from the womb whether his parents really want him.

Because the Moon lies sunk within the secretive eighth house, Jimi's more profound relationships are hard to decipher, his emotions hidden behind a facade of control. Jimi craved trusting and loving relationships, while demanding the independence to fly beyond the realms of ordinary mortals. Perversely, he became insanely jealous if anyone abandoned him.

The remaining celestial phenomenon in the eighth house is the chart's North Node, Jimi's point of karma, which is conjunct the planetoid Chiron. In Greek myth, Chiron, the centaur son of Saturn, is 'the wounded healer', an 'immortal' with musical and healing gifts. As part of his destiny, Jimi felt compelled to try and assuage his generation's collective pain.

Neptune In Libra: I can hear Atlantis full of cheer

At the top of the chart sits Neptune in Libra. Like Uranus and Pluto, Neptune falls beyond the boundaries of Saturn. The three outer planets represent the ideas, visions and feelings of generations rather than those of individuals; they are 'transpersonal'.

Neptune, ruler of the deep, personifies the collective dream. In such a prominent position, Neptune invited the hippie generation to project their collective fantasies onto Jimi. Neptune, strongly aspected by Sun and Moon, is a natural conduit for the fantasies of others; Jimi became a willing mirror for the peaceful ideals and vanities of the sixties generation.

The energy of Neptune is diffuse; this is the planet of dreams and sleep, and of the drugs that induce them, be they ether, alcohol or opium. It is also the planet of mysticism. Jimi's Neptunian links consume his chart, making its dominant theme his search for spiritual consciousness. Jimi Hendrix was carried along on Neptune's tides, mystically in touch with the Divine, yet swept away in a drug-induced miasma.

The cusp of the tenth house, the career point, lies in Libra, showing Jimi needed a balanced partnership to take him to the heights to which he aspired. Commercial success came when he struck such a partnership with the able Chas Chandler, though he appears to have lost the balance with co-manager, Mike Jeffery.

Mars in The Eleventh: Where you going with that gun in your hand?

The fireball Mars – "the instigator, the primordial activist" according to psychologist James Hillman – is in the freedom-oriented eleventh house, another sign of Jimi's rebellious nature, and Mars in the sexually charged sign of Scorpio gives Jimi's rebellion an outrageous, sexy, flamboyance. Ever the sexual conqueror off stage, on stage Jimi left no phallic nuance unexplored, stroking, thrusting, and going down on his guitar, and copulating with his amplifiers.

Mars in its own sign of Scorpio is also the mark of the soldier, and Jimi's decision to sign up for the forces in 1961 was a natural choice. That he joined the 101st Airborne parachute company – the "Screaming Eagles" – chimes with Mars' position

Feelin', sweet feelin' drops from my fingers,

Manic Depression is a catchin' my soul

Feelin', sweet feelin' drops from my fingers,

Woman so weary, the sweet cause in vain.

You make love, you break love,

Manic Depression is a

it's all the same when it's, when it's over

Music sweet music,

I wish I could caress, caress, caress

Woman so weary, the sweet cause in vain.

Manic Depression is a frustrating mess

You make love, you break love,

guitar

Cry on,

it's all the same when it's, when

Clip: Wild Thing .M [1]

Music sweet music,

I wish I could caress, caress, caress

Clip: Wild Thing .M [1]

Manic Depression is a

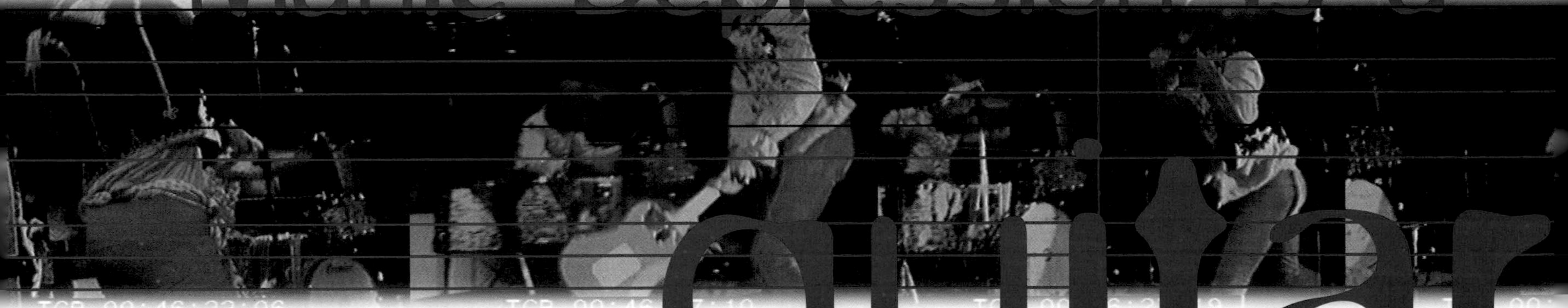

Cry on, guitar

Manic Depression is a catchin' my soul
Woman so weary, the sweet cause in vain.
You make love, you break love,
it's all the same when it's, when it's over
Clip: Foxy Lady .M [1]
Music sweet music
I wish I could caress, caress, caress
Manic Depression is a frustrating mess
catchin my soul
Cry on, guitar
it's over
frustrating mess

Foxy Lady (1970) Photograph : John Adler

"We'd step outside the stage door to where the teeny-boppers were and think, Oh, they won't bother about us and get torn apart! A girl was hanging on to my guitar saying, 'You don't want it.' I said to her, 'You MUST be out of your mind!'"

Backstage at the LA Forum on April 25, the opening date of the Cry Of Love tour. It is said that the inspiration for Foxy Lady was Heather Taylor who would later marry the Who's Roger Daltrey.

in Scorpio (whose symbol is the eagle as well as the scorpion) and in the eleventh house, an air house corresponding to the aviation-loving sign of Aquarius. "Kiss the Sky" was no idle fantasy for Jimi; he'd already tried to do exactly that.

The martial strains sounded strongly for James Marshall Hendrix. He and the US army divorced by mutual consent after a year, but he remained a warrior, with the guitar as his "Machine Gun". Although an icon for the peace and love generation, Jimi retained empathy for the common soldier; he would dedicate songs to both draft dodgers and to those on active service in Vietnam, fighting what Jimi believed was a just war. In turn, Hendrix's stratospheric guitars became part of the Vietnam war's soundtrack.

And The Gods Made Love – Planetary Aspects

Astrology holds the planets' relationships with each other – the aspects – are critical when examining the inner dynamics of the psyche. An aspect tells us whether the relationship, be it conscious or unconscious, is easy or difficult.

In Jimi's chart the opposition between his three Sagittarian planets in the twelfth house and the Saturn-Uranus conjunction in Gemini in the sixth is the axis which contains the rest of his bowl-shaped planetary activity.

The Sun-Saturn struggle suggests that the battle between Jimi's Sagittarian spirit and his strong-willed father, Al, symbolised by Saturn, was long-term and intense. While Al Hendrix succeeded in imparting a sense of discipline to his son, freedom remained the over-riding issue for Jimi, who after a short time working as handyman for his father, left home early in order to clarify his sense of self.

Jimi's Sagittarian impulse to travel was in part an act of self-definition, a symbolic departure from both father and fatherland. It was in London that Jimi Hendrix made his first record.

The conflict between Saturn in the house of duty and the Sun in the house of ancestors shows Jimi felt a strong need to rediscover, or reinvent, some kind of heritage for himself. We have already noted the strong call of the blues tradition on Jimi's playing. His feel for the deep rural blues of the 1920s as well as the electric blues of the forties and fifties was as effortless as it was obsessive.

Although he was only 'one-sixteenth' Cherokee, Jimi's Native American heritage also exercised a powerful call on him from an early age, and found its way into his artistic persona in songs like "One Rainy Wish" and in his love of Indian jewellery, where turquoise, the Sagittarian gemstone, was particularly prominent.

The Lights: Up from the skies

The "lights", the Sun and Moon, are central in any birth chart, but in Hendrix's case they exert an extraordinary authority. Both conjunct (ie adjoin) other planets, and both share an intense communion with each other through their harmonious, 120 degree (trine) aspect.

Furthermore, both Sun, symbolising the spirit, and Moon, symbolising the soul, fall into those areas of the chart – the twelfth and eighth house respectively – which are connected to mysticism, psychic powers and other "hidden" worlds. The marriage of spirit and soul represents an all pervasive, universal love – what Christian mystics call agap.

Jimi's Sun and Moon make direct associations with all three outer "generational" planets – Uranus, Neptune and Pluto – an unusual celestial seal heralding a man deeply in tune with his peers. This connection to the transpersonal planets makes Jimi a symbol of the hippie era.

The easy sextile aspect between Sun and Moon suggests that, although the marriage between Jimi's parents broke up, he really was a love child, the product of an intensely romantic union. Nevertheless, the conflicts between Al Hendrix and Lucille meant they parted when Jimi was seven (astrologers will note this is the time of his first Saturn square, a Uranus semi-sextile, and a progressed Moon square).

Venus-Uranus/Saturn: Love or Confusion?

The comfortable Sun-Moon relations further reflect a comfortable connection with both the male and female sides of Jimi's personality, or in Jungian terms, the Animus and Anima. For all his racy, macho qualities, Jimi dressed and even spoke in a soft, feminine way.

Despite Jimi's ease around women, the opposition of Uranus-Saturn to Venus, Mercury and Sun shows just how screwed-up were his relationships with women. The opposed Venus points to a series of grizzly love affairs, while Uranus adds a touch of sexual perversion.

The Venus-Uranus conflict is what the late astrologer Howard Sasportas would call the closeness-freedom dilemma. Venus wants to cuddle up while Uranus wants to spontaneously take off, "Stone Free", to become involved with wider concerns. The ability to give and receive unconditional love with one person was never in Jimi's make-up. In fact, he was

drawn to weird and crazy women – electric ladies, as he called them – precisely so he could keep his distance and avoid intimacy. A lyric like "So you say you want to be married, put me on a chain? You must be losing your weak little mind." ("51st Anniversary") is a good indicator of Jimi's attitude.

At times Jimi found it impossible not to be extremely cruel to girlfriends who tried to conquer his fear of one-to-one commitment. The Mercury-Venus conjunction suggests he thought constantly of love, and that Venus, the "Love Goddess", found in Jimi a willing herald. But the loss of his mother, and his own inability to love a special woman as much as he loved her, or indeed "Mother Earth" (the image appears repeatedly), thwarted every potential love affair.

To further complicate love matters, Venus in strong trine (120) aspect to Pluto emphasises extreme shifts of affection, changing Jimi without warning from beauty to beast, from lover and sex teacher to a venomous prince of darkness. This was a risk any woman who sought familiarity would have to chance.

Because Jimi's Mercury-Sun-Venus "band of gypsies" connect strongly to both Neptune and Pluto, the solution to many of the issues surrounding his parents, and his inability to hold down traditional love affairs, lay in his access to worlds beyond this one; the realm of archetypes, described by William Blake as "the wonders Divine of Human Imagination". These were the worlds which Jimi Hendrix briefly showed his fellow mortals, and which gave his work such abiding potency.

Jimi's Death : A surpise attack killed him in his sleep

Numerous astrological configurations show the death of Jimi Hendrix to be accidental, not intentional. Sagittarians are prone to extravagance and taking risks, and Hendrix chanced more than most. Jimi's strong Neptunian influence made it all too easy for him to lose himself in druggy oblivion, and to him the nine sleeping pills he took on the fateful night of September 17 / 18 wouldn't necessarily have seemed extravagant.

Health issues are evident within Jimi's horoscope. Uranus brings sudden disruptions to a body-conscious sixth house Saturn in Gemini, the air sign that rules lungs and windpipe. The planetary transits on the night of the 17th (transits show where planets are in relation to the natal horoscope) have Mercury and Mars in Virgo – respectively mind and body seeking good health – forming a triangular "T-square" aspect with the natal Uranus/Saturn and the Sagittarian planets.

A T-square transit indicates a critical time. The transiting Virgo planets disrupt the life force of the Sun and unsettle the "Time Lord" Saturn in Gemini, who abruptly limits the life's breath.

Interestingly, when Hendrix left the earthly plane, transiting Sun and Moon both formed tense aspects, constellating his need for spiritual contact, but instead of seeking a meditative union, Jimi chose to pop more pills. A progressed Mars in the twelfth house of self-undoing also indicates Jimi had become his own worst enemy. This passing phase could have been creative had Jimi given himself the seclusion to develop his spiritual disposition.

But for Jimi Hendrix solitude was hard to come by. Everyone wanted a piece of him and his action, and he found it hard to refuse them. The indications are that he had become irritated by his non-stop mental activity and the constant intrusions into his life. On September 18, 1970, Jimi just wanted to sleep.

Strange beautiful grass of green, with your majestic silver seas.
Your mysterious mountains I wish to see closer. May I land my kinky machine?

Although your world wonders me with your majestic and superior cackling hen.
Your people I do not understand, so to you I shall put an end.
You'll never hear surf music again.

(Third Stone From The Sun)

November 14, 1967

Rehearsals : Royal Albert Hall, London.

Photograph : Val Wilmer

Excuse me while I see
If the gypsy in me is right
If you don't mind
Well he signals me okay
So I think it's safe to say,
I'm gonna make a play

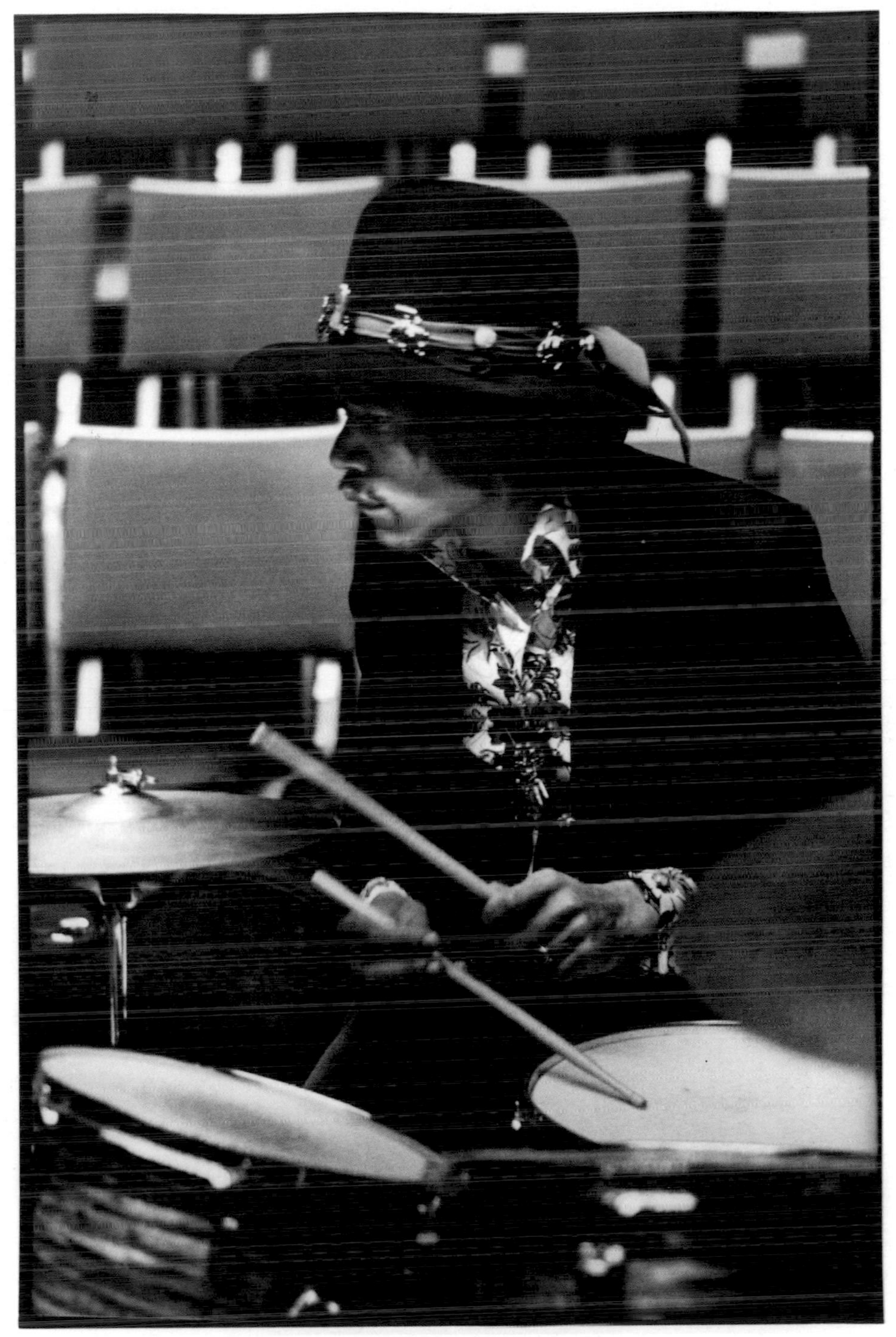

[August 1965, letter home] Nowadays people don't want you to sing good. They want you to sing sloppy and have a good beat to your songs. That's what angle I'm going to shoot for.

I got a break playing guitar for John Hammond Jr at the Cafe Au Go Go. That was great because the ceiling was really low and dusty. I'd stick the guitar right up into the ceiling. It was like war.

So I went back to New York and played with this little rhythm and blues group named Curtis Knight and the Squires.

My big slice of luck came when a little English friend persuaded Chas Chandler, the bass player of the Animals, to come down where we were gigging and give an ear. The Animals were doing their last gig as a group in Central Park. So Chas came down and heard me and asked would I like to come over to England and start a group there.

The way I write things they are just a clash between reality and fantasy. You have to use fantasy to show different sides of reality.

Photograph : Rancurel / Lampard

four other injured men to safety. For his actions he was awarded America's third highest military decoration, the Silver Star, for bravery under hostile fire.

In rehab, Buddy "heard Jimi in Camp Drake Evac Hospital in Tokyo where I was in the spinal cord neuro-surgery ward". Manic depression captured my soul ... you don't look like you used to. "That place was without a doubt the most terrible experience I've ever endured. We played Hendrix as we drag raced all night on motorised wheelchairs. We got thoroughly fucked up and listened to Hendrix all night long. For me, that was like medicine. That was the cure."

Back in the world "every place I went, every head's house, crash pad, every place had Hendrix posters and albums. 'See that guy? That's who we are. That's where we're goin'. That's us there.'" Not necessarily stoned, but beautiful.

Michael Herr's Dispatches says it all: Vietnam was the first "rock'n'roll war", and Jimi was its forward scout. His music was everywhere. Not so much on the bland, censorious and programmed-from-Washington AFVN (the Armed Forces Vietnam Network), but on tapes sent by stateside friends and lovers, hoarded like morphine to deaden the constant pain. There was the distant machine-gun rat-tat-tat opening of "Waterfall: Will I live tomorrow? Well I just can't say. It's a shame to waste your time away like this." The casual violence of "Hey, Joe! Where you goin' with that gun in your hand?" And Joe's answer, no less urgent, that "I'm stone free to do what I please. I got to got to got to get away right now!"

But there was nowhere to run, nowhere to hide. The enemy was everywhere, and sometimes, in a roomful of mirrors, we met the enemy and he was us.

Lately things don't seem the same.

Art : Waldemar Swierzy

During the TET Offensive, in February 1968, the "enemy" launched major attacks on more than six dozen provincial capitals, bases, and Saigon itself, where communist troops captured and held the American Embassy for seven hours. A few blocks away stood one of the primest targets in the war, the three-hundred-foot-tall broadcast tower of the American Armed Forces radio and television stations. All along the watchtower, halfway up, a Vietnamese guard sat on a couple of planks of wood laid across the structure's spidery steel beams. He was the only one supposed to be up there, but, for a couple of bottles of Ba Moui Ba (Bière 33, the local brew which had been analysed and found to contain formaldehyde), or a few joints, the hapless soldier would turn a blind eye to anyone stupid enough to want to scale the heights.

And what heights they were! A perfect 360 of the wickedest light show west of the Fillmore. To the south, in the delta, came waves of low-flying napalm strikes, whose wake left billowing scarlet, gold and black fireclouds of roiling fury. To the west and north, tracer fire etched laser-red morse-code dashes against the hazy blackness of the night-time sky. Buildings exploded in white-silver frenzy on the eastern horizon. A chopper fell in fuel-fed flame, a purple haze all in my brain.

"There ain't no life nowhere! But … are you experienced? Well, I am!" Jimi on the box, thirty storeys up, everything immediate, yet distanced. Jimi's chords locked in aerial dogfights, gliding, riding, sliding, hiding, belligerent bursts, hallucinogenic, a head-warping face-wiping mind melt, chords like dive-bombers screaming in for the kill, scintillating, serrated chords shot through with arc-light shrieks of staccato mayhem, as immediate and horrific as the firefight racketing away this very second below our red and puffy eyes; chords that hang in the air like the retinal retention of an eerie afterburn, the stars displaced and the smell of a world that is burned. Overhead, night birds flying, Huey, Apache, Chinook, wooshing with murderous potential. And over everything, every apocalyptic bang, boom and rattle – Jimi, bleating like Braxton and bonding with the bombast.

Sometimes, sodden with drink, or stretched out in an opium haze, Saigon troops would stagger down Tu Do, the Graham Greene street of commercial affection, past bars whose fragile doors would slap open, and emit a blast of music from their clamorous, cloudy interiors. The live bands were pan-Asian; here a Flip-rock combo or a Taiwanese duo, there a third-rate, cheesy Thai band, all of them mangling the words. "Freedom to live! Freedom, that's what I need," only it came out "fleadom". Even worse to hear them sing "Pul-purr haze oar in my blain", but it was beyond pathetic when they bleated "God bress Amelica, rand that I rub", and all the GIs would stand up with their cunt-caps over their hearts, many of them collapsing in tears. I taste tears and a whole lot of precious tears wasted. Sirens flashing with earth and rock and stone.

Saigon: where Ho meant an uncle, not a lover.

Down in the delta, swampy home of the most dedicated communist guerillas, there was an old lady named Maria who had the best grass in IV Corps. She lived a short drive from Can Tho, in an area that was owned at night by Victor Charles.

Maria was able to cross the invisible lines of war and trade with the local VC herb growers. She was famous throughout the south for her blend, as fine a medley of maryjane as I've ever encountered to this day. Don't let your imagination take you by surprise. One variety got you off on the first hit; another was pure smokin' psychedelia, roasty-toasty and hypnotic; the third was like hamburger helper, and served to extend the high for what seemed like hours.

But Maria was expensive too. Unlike the cartons of 200 reloaded Park Lanes you could pick up from any Saigon pedicab driver for two bucks US, she charged an unheard of $15 per kilo for her primo, packed in official US government 2.2 pound regulation sandbags.

The local troops all agreed the investment was worth it.

Part of the fun of dealing with Maria was watching her delight as the ground-poundin' grunts, fresh from their latest decimation, lay back to sample her wares. She had a little tin-speakered Aiwa cassette player set atop sacks of stash, and from it a jarring parade of doper hits jangled relentlessly. Head resting with Jimi: now if you would excuse me I must be on my way.

Once I saw a cocky short-timer introduce a clueless newby to Maria's ferocious flora, and he had to be carried to his deuce-and-a-half and tossed in the back, so heavy was the hit. Sometimes I can feel my heart runnin' kinda hot.

Maria would just smile her wrinkled and secret smile, doing her little bit to bring the war to a quicker conclusion, all the while provoking our spirits with the pneumatic breathing of "Purple Haze", its ending a wild shrill of shrapnel bells.

WORDS OF WOE/WORDS OF WAR
bucu/ titi/ number ten/ steam and cream/ cacadao you GI/ locked, cocked and ready to rock/ General/ Private/ Colonel/ A Public Affairs Center without one Colonel of Truth in the whole building/ filthy urchins didimao-ing with the wallet of some dumb REMF (rear echelon mother fucker)/ bombard/ mutilate/ decimate/ annihilate/ pestilence/ horrific/ apocalypse/ assault/ patrol/ search and destroy/ DMZ/ LZ/ brass/ non-com/ TDY to Hell – temporary duty to oblivion/ offshore/ strafe/ bloop/ batter/ battle/ bombastic/ on-target/ catapult/ courageous/ dutiful/ obedient/ harsh/ insistent/ maimed/ blasted/ blown away/ barrage/ brigade/ grunt/ ground-pounder/ straight-leg/ frag/ flags/ DEROS/ short/ short time/ swagger stick/ punji stick/ NVA/ Cong/ Charlie/ slits/ slopes/ slanty-eyed motherfuckers/ gooks/ newby.

Lifer!

Spec 4 Jack Martin had been a commercial artist in civilian life, painting with lifelike precision a series of book jackets, album covers, and magazine illustrations. The army decided to use his talents to sketch primitive propaganda leaflets for the Fourth PsyOps Group headquarters in Saigon. PsyOps is where they put the mutants, the misfits, the drafted PhD candidates who refused to become officers. It had the highest average IQ of any unit in the country, and the group was hated for it. Its detractors needn't have worried, however: PsyOps was as wigged-out, lame and confused as the most optimistic Hanoi Red could have hoped.

Jack was ordered to design a leaflet that portrayed a young Vietnamese woman in a skimpy bikini with the words "Look who's waiting for you when you surrender to our side" printed over her near-naked body. The Vietnamese, being a very modest, almost prudish, people, were appalled by the image. The words themselves had almost no chance of influencing the hard-core Cong fighters; the leaflet was just further proof to them of the depravity and ignorance of the American invaders. None of them along the line know what any of it is worth.

Each day as he laboured at his drawing board in the rear of a quonset hut in a former railyard in downtown Saigon, Jack would play Hendrix music on his Akai reel-to-reel recorder. "Jimi was the point at which you went inside, and stopped listening to the bastards in charge. He was the guy who wore the flowered shirt and didn't look like a sissy; he taught us how to dress. He played the guitar all wrong, he held it upside down and backwards, so he broke all the rules, everything about him was extreme – just like us. Everything was too much in the Nam.

"You couldn't separate acid from Jimi, he represented a way to listen to the sound of your own outer limits. Being there and listening to him, no matter what the kids back home thought his music meant, they could never connect at the level we did. We were in the right zone to tune in. More intensity, more extremism. When we got back to the world, it was the soundtrack of the war, and if you tried to communciate that to people here, you couldn't make them understand, they thought you were crazy." You'll probably scream and cry.

"All those people dying: Presidents, students, soldiers, Janis, black leaders, they all merge in memory now. All those words – Puff the Magic Dragon – back in the States it was symbolism, but here it was happening."

Art : Rob O'Connor for Stylorouge - Courtesy Pictor International / Uniphoto

You couldn't drop out in Nam, you were already dropped, and no matter what you dropped, you were already on the bottom.

"On the other hand, Jimi kept us strong in our idealism – because we were right and he said so. For a while all the souls wanted to have a 'fro like Jimi's, and lots of them wore wigs off duty. He brought the races together with the consciousness behind the music, and his lyrics. Maybe it's just a change of climate. I saw that right from my first night in country. I pulled guard duty, and everywhere I went, everyone was out looking for a place to get high. All I could smell as I marched around all night was marijuana, and all I could hear was Hendrix playin' in the jungle under the trees.

"In the art hut, I was put in the very back by a wall. So I had them install a translucent plexiglass panel next to my desk, so I could try to get some natural light. I was at the end point of the constant trickle of crap created by some dumb committee. It just took a few months before me and the other guys started to fight them. The Star (slowly strangled) Banner. All of us making fun of the idiot lieutenant in charge, even the Vietnamese (whose lives depended on him).

"There was this real angry PFC who was always getting in trouble, always gettin' busted, a guy named Nelson. He eventually built an eight-foot-high enclosure around his desk with cardboard boxes – and that's all we ever saw of him. One day the inspector-general came to check out our unit, and everybody was completely uptight. When the guy saw Nelson's billet, frail and most unregulation, he was about to hit the ceiling when Mr Thanh, the ever-smiling and most willing to oblige among the 'host national' artists we employed, grabbed his sketch pad and began drawing wonderfully accurate caricatures of the IG and his staff. They were not only distracted, but charmed."

Eventually, Jack punched two holes through the corrugated panel against which he sat. One was attached to a tube that was the right diameter to hold a joint; the other empty, so "I could keep the smoke outdoors." The classified material burn barrel was just behind the hut, and a steady stream of EM came out to smoke Park Lanes around it, the acrid stink of burning diesel fuel masking the pot's perfume. Someone would insert a joint in Jack's tube, tap twice on the wall to announce lift-off, and Jack stayed stoned for the entire war. "I was like twenty feet away from this dumb-ass second lieutenant, and the guy was so zoned he didn't even realise what I was doing." There are many among us who feel that life is but a joke. "Even the Vietnamese guys began to get hip – popping out to the latrine with their 'Vietnamese tobacco'. Twenty hits later they'd wink at the round-eyes at the barrels, and come back inside wired to the gills. Lord I gotta leave this town … I hear my train a-comin'."

Eighty miles south of Saigon lay one of the most peaceful places on earth, right in the middle of the Mekong River, in the very heart of the war. It was an island – sandbar, really – called Con Phuong, the Island of the Coconut Monk.

Here lived thousands of people in complete peace and serenity in a kind of religious Disneyland, led by a four and a half-foot-tall hunchback monk who hadn't lain down since 1932. There were deserters from both the North and the South Vietnamese armies, Taoist pacifists, even a handful of American deserters, and supporters like John Steinbeck IV, who brought me there for the first of my seven visits. Anyone who arrived without a weapon was welcomed, no questions asked. Everybody! We got to live together!

The Americans controlled the north bank of the river; the communists, the south. They fired rockets and mortars back and forth over the island, but never touched the island itself. Saigon let it exist because it was safer to have all the dissenters stuck down there, where they could be kept under surveillance, than have them burning themselves alive on the streets of the capital before the consuming cameras of the international press. I swear I seen nothin' but a lot of frowns. Con Phuong was the only place in my twenty-six months in Nam that I saw truly happy people. Every three hours, both day and night, each family would send one representative to pray for peace on a huge circular platform built on stilts at the tip of the island. They knelt among gaily painted icons and statues; Christ shaking hands with Buddha, the Virgin Mary clasping Kwan Yin, Lao Tse straddling the world. They prayed to all of them: Christ, Buddha, Mohammed, Lao Tse, Confucius, even Sun Yat Sen, Victor Hugo and Winston Churchill.

The platform had nine tall columns, each of them capped with a pink lotus blossom, and surrounded by a swirling yellow dragon, the symbol of Vietnam. Everything on the island seemed to have a double or triple meaning. The number nine was deeply important to the devotees because the Mekong, composed of nine tributaries, was known as the River of the Nine Dragons. It was also the Trinity times itself, as young English-speaking "monks" would tell the visitors who came in abundance from all over the world.

Also astraddle the prayer platform was a double bell tower manned constantly by purple-robed youths who took shifts slamming suspended eight-foot-long tree trunks into massive bells made from melted-down American shell casings. This they had vowed to do until the war was finally over, and the haunting, taunting echoes of their strikes reverberated up and down river ceaselessly, day and night.

The riverine ambience was as bizarre as the last half-hour of *Apocalypse Now*, the Brando scenes, only it was the polar and peaceful opposite of that fantasy. In fact, the only serious incident the island had experienced was when some macho American chopper pilot dropped tear gas on the worshippers at a Sunday noon prayer service, because he hated "peace creeps", providing me with another nail in the coffin of my patriotism.

Dao Dua, as the Coconut Monk was called, was a wispy, diminutive figure in golden robes, descended from some mythological realm. In the 1920s he had been sent to France to be educated as a chemical engineer, in the hopes that he would become a functionary for the colonial oppressor. Instead, he returned and started living like a flagpole sitter, perched high atop a coconut palm, fasting and praying for deliverance – first from the French, then from the Japanese, and now from the Americans. In the early sixties, a wealthy Chinese benefactor had given him the island, and by the end of the decade there were perhaps 5,000 people who'd

Isn't it nice to be alive
says the GI
As he wipes the mud from his eyes
and the shells fly
Way past, below and overhead
My tears roll down through the valleys
as they burn everything and leave

dropped out of the war to come live in communal bliss with him. Each was given a house to live in, built by the community. Labour, and everything else, was shared among the island's denizens in a dramatic display of pure spiritual communism.

Here, we felt the spirit of Jimi omnipresent, whether lying on our backs listening to his tapes underneath the booming five-ton bells, our brains fried on acid; or sitting cross-legged in a meditation chamber beneath a psychedelically painted portrait of the monk, with its multicoloured swirly words "Why Is This Man Smiling?" leading our minds along a myriad of potential pathways. Do you really want to be experienced?

We were actually in the place that was the light at the end of the tunnel, the peace-filled centre of our dreams, while all around us the world was in a state of permanent "drain bamage", the phrase of Tim Page, the finest (and most wounded) Vietnam combat photographer, himself a frequent seeker in this haven of peace.

It was Page who insisted that one could not take the glamour out of war. Blown apart five times, Page became the celebrant of salacious sensations, documenter of the South-East Asian demi-monde of death and finality. Let him have the final word: "Vietnam," he said, "is what we had instead of happy childhoods."

I was so cold and lonely, the rain was tearin' me up ... I ain't comin' down this lonely road again.

Photograph : Douglas Kent Hall (1969)

On September 5 Jimi debuted "Machine Gun" at this street festival in Harlem. The sound of war and chaos held special significance for Jimi and the inner-city blacks because of the lopsided percentage of black GIs sent to Vietnam's front line - Soulville.

"Sometimes when I come up here people say, 'He plays white rock for white people. What's he doin' here?' Well, I want to show them that music is universal, there is no white rock or black rock. Some of these kids haven't got $6.00 to go to Madison Square Garden. Music is stronger than politics. I feel sorry for the minorities but I don't feel a part of one. And I think the answer lies in music. Forget about the mass love scene, it's not building understanding. I wish I could say this so strongly that they'd sit up in their chairs."

Down the street you can hear her scream, "You're a disgrace..."
As she slams the door in his drunken face
And now he stands outside and all the neighbours start to gossip and drool.
He cries, "Oh girl, you must be mad, what happened to the sweet love you and me had?"
Against the door he leans and starts a scene and his tears fall and burn the garden green.

A little Indian brave who, before he was ten, played war games in the woods with his Indian friends,
and he built a dream that when he grew up he would be a fearless warrior Indian Chief.
Many moons passed and more
The dream grew strong
until tomorrow he would sing his first war song
and fight his first battle.
But something went wrong,
surprise attack killed him in his sleep that night.

There was a young girl whose heart was a frown
Cause she was crippled for life and she couldn't speak a sound
And she wished and prayed she could stop living
So she decided to die
She drew her wheelchair to the edge of the shore
And to her legs she smiled
"You won't hurt me no more"
But then a sight she'd never seen made her jump and say
"Look, a golden winged ship is passing my way."

And so castles made of sand melt into the sea, eventually
(Castles Made Of Sand)

Photograph : Jean-Pierre Leloir

BORN ON THE FOURTH OF JULY

It was in January 1968. I was transfered up to the north. Some of the bunkers - only about ten per cent of them at this time - had guys in them who'd be smoking grass and listening to rock - the Doors and Jefferson Airplane, particularly. These were the heads, and this was the first place I really remember hearing Jimi's guitarplaying, which shocked me; I was into classical music before this. His guitar was so dissonant, and the lyrics - even though at first it was difficult to hear what he was singing about - were of a kind that had not been heard before. It was not normal music at all, definitely acid music and you could also tell that Jimi was a head.

There was a whole contingent of black guys there who dug soul. A lot of them didn't really like him. But the ones who smoked grass did - Jimi crossed those dividing lines: a lot of the black druggies really understood his guitar style; they also appreciated the fact that he managed to look so great and be ex-army at the same time. In fact, soul music was not very popular with the white guys. Although the heads also listened to a lot of black jazz - Thelonius Monk, Manu Dibango, people like that. My head was going round completely on this stuff. I was doing acid and being born again.

During the course of 1968, Jimi became more popular. There was something about his music that was very much a downer, and it fitted with what was going on out there. Everyone was becoming increasingly frustrated, but combat proved a unifying experience.

Freedom was an important concept for everyone there, and Jimi evoked a sense of breaking to another reality. By those who knew of him he was certainly considered one of the brothers.

Oliver Stone

Photograph : Joel Axelrad / Retna

1983 - A mermaid I should
Turn To Be -

Hooray, I awake from yesterday
alive, But the war is here to stay
So my love, Catherina and me, decide
to take our last walk to the sea
Not to die but to be re-born away from
lands so battered and torn forever
Oh Sea, it is really such a mess, every inch
of earth is a fighting nest. pencil and
lipstick tube shaped things, continue
to rain and cause pain and stain
and the artic melts from blue to red,
As our feet finds the sand and the
sea's just up ahead

The brilliant glamour of the Empire State Building piercing the twilight of the sky over the myriad colored lights of New York.

Dear Dad -
Well --- I'm just dropping in
a few words to let you know
everything's so-so here in this big
raggedy city of New York - Everything's
happening bad here - I hope
every one at home is alright.
tell Leon I said Hello - I'll write
you a letter real soon - And will
Try to send a decent picture -
So until then I hope you're doing
alright, tell Ernie I play the
blues like they NEVER heard - Love always, Jimmy

POST CARD
Address
Mr. James Allen Hendrix
2606 E Yesler Way
Seattle. Wash.
98122

to Danielle
(a very Sweet girl)
Love always
Jimi Hendrix

The morning is dead / And the day is too / The step is up here to meet me / But the velvet fool / All my loneliness / I have felt today

It's a little more than enough today / To make a man throw himself away / I continue to burn the midnight lamp alone

Now the smiling portrait of you / Is still hanging on my frowning wall / It really doesn't, really doesn't bother me to watch at all / It's just the ever falling dust that makes it so hard for me to see

Lonely lonely lonely / Loneliness is such a drag

Soon enough time will tell / About the circus and the wishing well

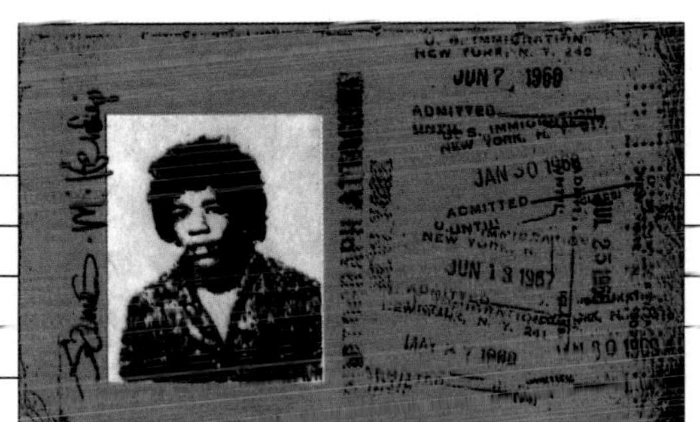

I won't be able to see you until about 2 months from now — Thats if I'm lucky — We're going through Basic Training, Thats the reason — Although I've been here for about a week, it seems like about a month — Time passes pretty slow even though we do have alot to do. —

How's the gardening business? I hope it's doing fine — I believe it's more expensive being in the Army than it is living as a civilian — So far we had to get —

1. 2 laundry bags 1.00 each, 2 black hat 1.75, 2 locks .80 each, 3 Towels .50 each, Stamping kit 1.75, Haircut 1.00, Shoe polish kit 1.70, Shaveing razor and blades and lather 1.70, insignias .50. So I guess this isn't all that good, finacially, as I first thought. $10.60 — that's about what it is. And, we have to buy way more than that before we're actually set for awhile, and we don't get paid until JUNE 30th 1961. And so I would like to know if you might be able to send about 5 or 6 dollars —

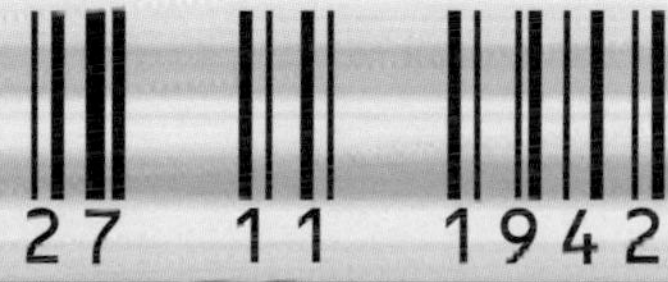

Photograph : Ron Rafaelli / Michael Ochs Archives (1968)
"Little Wing was a very sweet girl that came around that gave me her whole life and more if I wanted it... and me with my crazy ass couldn't get it together."

NEWPORT
Menthol

Burberry Blues

At the audition it was strange. I met this black guy with very, very wild hair wearing this Burberry raincoat. He looked very straight really, apart from his hair. We didn't talk much at first - you've got to remember this was an audition for me sandwiched in between two sessions. Jimi was very soft-spoken and gave the impression of being very gentle, almost shy. It was immediately apparent that he was a good guitarist; but at this stage I was more knocked out that he could cover so many different styles as well. You name it he could do it. I think we did "Have Mercy Babe" first. Jimi didn't really sing, more mumbled along to the music - Chas really had to coax it out of him. But we both clearly loved the same types of music.

Mitch Mitchell

Photograph : Jean-Noel Coghe

TCR 00:10:39:07
TCR 00:10:39:18
TCR 00:10:40:14
TCR 10:01:57:06
TCR 10:01:56:16
TCR 10:01:55:06

TCR 10:01:53:21
TCR 10:01:57:23
TCR 10:01:57:20

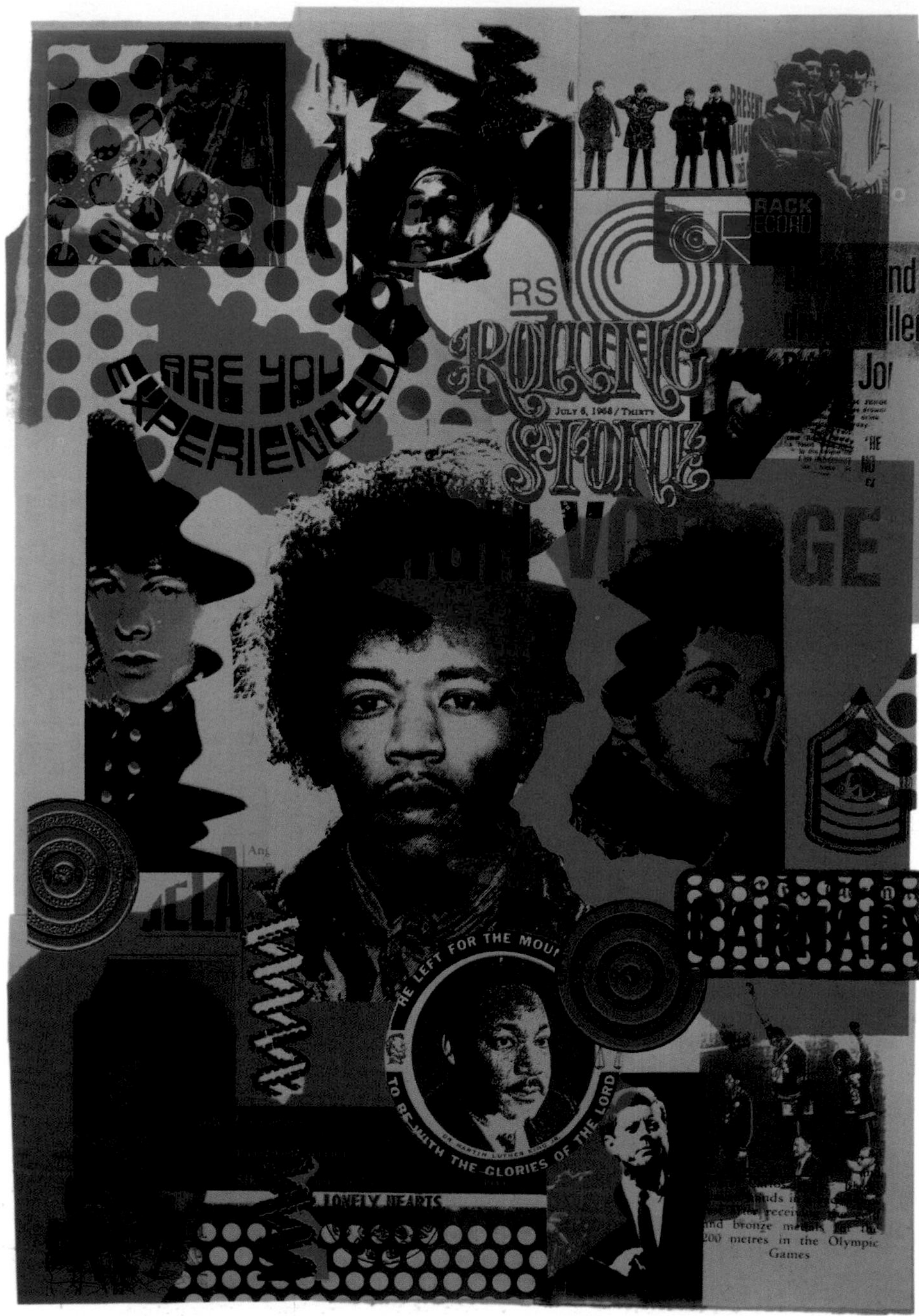

"It's me, Jimmy. I'm in England, Dad. I met some people and they're going to make me a big star. We changed my name to J-I-M-I."

"I arrived in Britain with just the suit I stood up in. I'm going back with the best wardrobe of gear that Carnaby Street can offer. Noel and Mitch will go great in the States. They'll love them so much they won't have to wash their own socks."

Shooting Stars (1992)
Art : Ian Wright

In 1964 Jimi moves for a time to New York City.

I went to New York and won first place in the Apollo amateur contest, you know, twenty-five dollars … So I stayed up there, starved up there for two or three weeks. I'd get a gig once every twelfth of never. Sleeping outside between them tall tenements was hell. Rats runnin' all over your chest, cockroaches stealin' your last candy bar from your very pockets. I even tried to eat orange peel and tomato paste.

I played with the Isley Brothers for a while and they used to make me do my thing, because it made them more bucks or something … Most groups I was with, they didn't let me do my own thing.

He is still on tour with the Isley Brothers who have dates to play there. In Manhattan he quits the group and lives briefly in Harlem. At Manny's Music Store on 48th Street Jimi buys his first Fender, a Duosonic. Even in the concrete canyons of Manhattan he is ethereal, spacy, intangible, as though he is still floating suspended on that magical parachute.

Then Jimi takes a job working for Sam Cooke with whom he stays almost until the singer's death in December 1964. He really learns soul music.

Back on the road he continues playing behind soul and r&b acts. He finds an ally in the Chicago bluesman Tommy Tucker, who has hit the charts with his song "High-Heel Sneakers". Back in Nashville he discovers a kinship with Steve Cropper and then with Albert King, another left-hander. Out on the package-tour circuit, he finally meets and receives instruction from BB King, a hero.

Playing again with Little Richard, Jimi decides to quit the tour once it reaches Los Angeles. While there, he encounters a hip black musician called Arthur Lee, then in the process of forming the group Love. Lee needs a guitarist to record a song of his for a single, "My Diary". And despite having given his notice in to Little Richard, the pompadoured one requests Jimi's licks on his next single for the Veejay label, "Don't Know What You've Got But It's Got Me", unfortunately destined to be the first Little Richard single to fail to make the charts.

Back with Little Richard for a spring tour, things come to a head when they hit New York in April 1965. Three dismal dates at the Paramount Theatre culminate in Little Richard being thrown off the bill; meanwhile, Jimi manages to miss the tour bus to Washington DC the next morning and is himself canned from the backing group.

It is the proverbial blessing in disguise. In New York Jimi's ambitions are properly focused by the music exploding out of the city. In Harlem he is confronted by the extraordinary sounds of the newest jazz. Jimi becomes a big fan of Roland Kirk and Ornette Coleman – especially of the Ornette Coleman album *Something Else* – and John Coltrane. Such work offers new sonic possibilities for Jimi's own music; a point of transition from his r&b roots. His day-to-day playing, however, is less artistically dramatic. Jimi takes a job with a small club band called Curtis Knight and the Squires, with whom he works for eight months. During that time he also tours with Joey Dee and the Starlighters, hitmakers with "Peppermint Twist" and house band at the Peppermint Lounge.

[August 1965, letter home] Nowadays people don't want you to sing good. They want you to sing sloppy and have a good beat to your songs. That's what angle I'm going to shoot for.

Jimi moves downtown to Greenwich Village, where he is influenced by the lyrical innovations of Bob Dylan that have changed the vocabulary of popular music – *Highway 61 Revisited* is a significant influence, and he begins to adopt a look like that of a black Dylan, his hair in particular taking on a look not dissimilar to the singer's. In 1966, following his last r&b sideman gig with the saxophonist King Curtis, Hendrix forms his own band and elects to sing for the first time. Away from the rigid confines of working as a background musician, Jimi Hendrix shapes a new blueprint for the future. The group is called Jimmy James and the Blue Flames and they have a regular spot at the Cafe Wha? in Greenwich Village. Word soon spreads about this extraordinary black guitarist who even plays with his teeth. It is unlike anything else, a glorious noise that subverts all notions of electric music.

One night Jimi Hendrix's show is watched by Chas Chandler, the former bass player with the Animals. Immediately overwhelmed by the sheer vivacity of Hendrix's performance, Chandler offers Jimi a management contract and invites him to London. The breakthrough has come.

On September 24, 1966, the quiet dynamic force of Jimi Hendrix arrives in London. On the first-class flight from New York, he and Chas Chandler have put their heads together and come up with the idea of changing his name from Jimmy to Jimi. Chas Chandler introduces him to hip England; and following an impromptu jam with Cream, Hendrix is a rising currency in London. With his loose velvet clothing and electric hair Jimi Hendrix looks as though he is bringing messages from Mars – which he possibly is.

In fact, he has come to England because he has no place else to go. Jimi Hendrix has no doubts whatsoever about his own abilities – the only problem he has is getting other people to recognise them. There he is, stuck in Manhattan, playing low funky clubs for no money at all, and all of a sudden Chas Chandler serves notice that he recognises his talent. The action is happening in England at this time. And here comes Chas saying let's go to England. Why the hell not?

The first priority is to form a group. Within a month Jimi Hendrix has found drummer Mitch Mitchell, formerly with Georgie Fame's Blue Flames. It is almost like divine providence: Mitch Mitchell is to prove the only drummer with whom Jimi will have a complete and total artistic empathy. A great love and respect develops between the two musicians – not only can Mitch keep up with Jimi's outlandish musical thinking, but Jimi will even listen when Mitch, as stubborn and musically violent as Jimi, disagrees with what the guitarist is trying to do. Jimi, who will intimidate almost all other musicians with whom he plays, is unable to have the same effect on Mitch Mitchell.

Guitarist turned bass player Noel Redding is also taken on, and the Jimi Hendrix Experience is officially formed on October 6, 1966. The following week they play a four-date French tour supporting Johnny Halliday, the Gallic Elvis.

On October 23, the band record their first two songs, "Hey Joe" and "Stone Free", at London's De Lane Lea Studios. The record is cut as an independent production and Chandler goes in search of a record deal. Incredibly, he is rejected by a number of companies before Polydor Records accept the single. When the record is released at the very end of 1966, the Jimi Hendrix Experience almost immediately become the hottest new group in Britain. "Hey Joe", which Chas Chandler has heard Jimi play in New York, is an explosion of primal sound and new rhythmic possibilities; the song has been a US pop hit for the Leaves – but Jimi slows the pace of the tune, slurring the vocal while hitting that rich guitar tone that comes to distinguish his work. "Underground rock" has just been born, and the record sets the Experience up as the standard-bearers for this new musical movement.

In the United Kingdom "Hey Joe" is released on December 16, 1966, its release coinciding with the group's debut on the second to last edition of the influential television show *Ready Steady Go!*. By February 1967, the record has reached number 4 in the charts. Its successor, "Purple Haze", gets to number

3; although this second single does not seem as instantly commercial as "Hey Joe", it is a stronger showcase for Jimi's talents – not only has Jimi written the song, but it shows how he can be both lead and rhythm player at the same time. "The Wind Cries Mary", the group's third hit, is a beautiful, plaintive ballad. And the trio's debut album, *Are You Experienced?*, is number 2 to the Beatles' *Sergeant Pepper* through the summer of 1967.

The time has come to introduce the United States to the Jimi Hendrix Experience. Word of the band's British success has percolated across the Atlantic and Warner Brothers snap up the US record deal.

In June the group travel to California to play at the Monterey International Pop Festival. This is a vast open-air concert, a celebration of the burgeoning alternative culture and focus of the Summer Of Love. The bill includes The Grateful Dead, Jefferson Airplane, Electric Flag, the Byrds, Ravi Shankar, Quicksilver Messenger Service, Country Joe and the Fish, the Steve Miller Band, Buffalo Springfield, Big Brother And the Holding Company, The Mamas and the Papas, Otis Redding and, from Britain, The Who and the Jimi Hendrix Experience.

(ERIC BURDON on JIMI at MONTEREY: "He crouched down in the sun, a silver conch belt around his hips, white calf-length boots, gypsy waistcoat, a purple shirt, the box of coloured inks and oils alongside his guitars. He was quite alone. I stood and watched a minute. It was like a Navaho dream – the warrior before the hunt.")

Jimi's appearance at the festival, moreover, comes courtesy of an important testimonial: that of Paul McCartney, one of the festival's "board of governors". In 1967 there can be no more credible recommendation, except possibly for an onstage introduction to the act by Jimi's friend Brian Jones – which duly takes place. The group's performance climaxes when, in a now celebrated moment, Jimi torches his guitar with lighter fluid as the group play "Wild Thing", a phenomenal version of a song previously associated with the British group, the Troggs. The performance of this song, as documented in DA Pennebaker's film of the festival, is one of the great moments in the history of rock – even though its effect is thoroughly calculated: "Make sure you've got plenty of film in your camera," Jimi advises photographer Jim Marshall before he goes on stage. More than anything, it is this show, culminating in the performance of "Wild Thing", that breaks Jimi in the United States. Jimi Hendrix walks out on to the stage unknown and leaves it a legend.

On the back of the white Fender he burns and tosses into the audience Jimi has inscribed a poem he has written:

May this be
Love or just
Confusion born out of
Frustration wracked
Feelings – of not
Being able to
Make true physical
Love to the universal gypsy queen
True, free expressed music
Darling guitar please rest.
Amen.

When Jimi sets his guitar alight at Monterey he is simply taking those chitlin circuit musical histrionics to their most logical extremity. Not only is Jimi a master musician, but he is also a supreme entertainer, capable of holding an audience in the palm of his hand. In time this particular ability of Jimi's will come to haunt him: he becomes deeply

Fire Works (1967) / Photograph : Ed Caraeff

Monterey: Jimi is announced by the Stones' Brian Jones as '... the most exciting performer I've ever heard...' Hendrix's set climaxed with an astonishing version of "Wild Thing" during which he pulled out every trick in the book: from playing behind his back to on his knees, from pummelling his guitar into submission to fucking against the speakers. The finale was almost an act of sacrifice as he squirted lighter fuel over the misshapen instrument and set fire to it. As his Stratocaster squawked its final death throes, Jimi hurled the remnants into the audience.

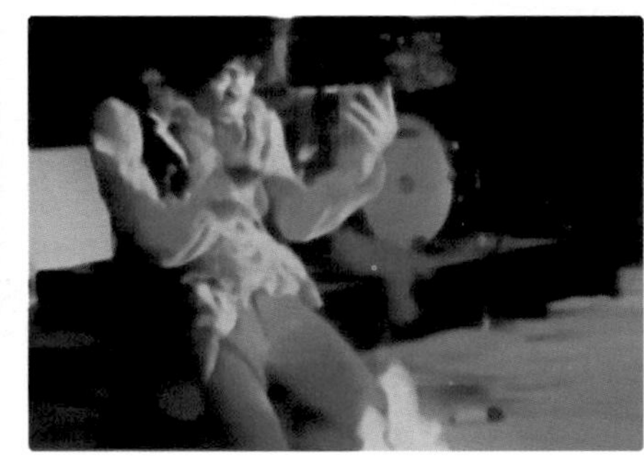

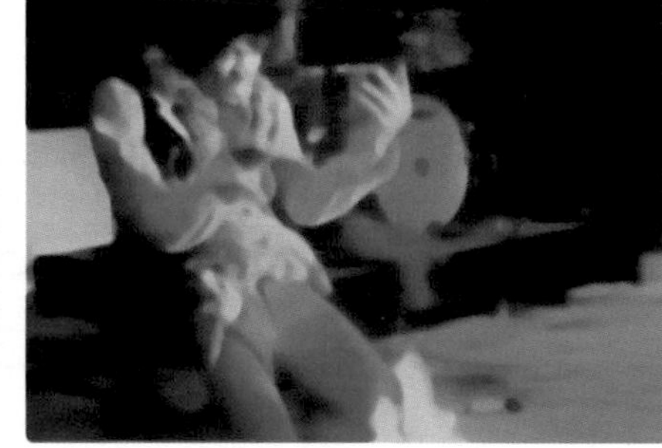

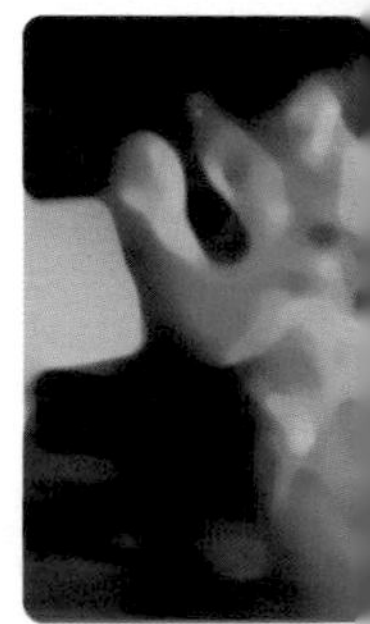

"The time I burned my guitar it was like a sacrifice. You sacrifice the things you love. I love my guitar. I'd just finished painting it that day and was really into it. When we played in the Hollywood Bowl they were waiting for us with fire extinguishers."

"The time I burned my guitar it was like a sacrifice. You sacrifice the things you love. I love my guitar. I'd just finished painting it that day and was really into it. When we played in the Hollywood Bowl they were waiting for us with fire extinguishers."

concerned that audiences are coming only to watch him, rather than listen to his music.

Following this US debut at Monterey, the Jimi Hendrix Experience become the hottest new act in the world. Jimi and the group, fuelled by adrenaline-fired energy, are flung into a maelstrom of concerts, recording, promotion, and travel. Despite offers from the hippest promoters, however, Hendrix's co-manager Mike Jeffery makes a strange decision: he books the band as support act on a tour by the Monkees, the manufactured group who cannot have been further in spirit from Jimi Hendrix. When the dates start it is obvious a mistake has been made. Eight days into the tour the Jimi Hendrix Experience make their excuses (blaming the right-wing Daughters Of The American Revolution) and leave. After a hastily arranged schedule of showcase concerts, including a week at San Francisco's Fillmore West, Hendrix and the group return to Britain in late August.

A new single, "The Burning Of The Midnight Lamp", is released; a song of extraordinary beauty and power, it has the strongest, most insidious melody of all the group's releases up until then. And on December 1, 1967, towards the end of their second British tour (the band's first as headline act) the Jimi Hendrix Experience release a new album. *Axis: Bold As Love* is looser than *Are You Experienced?* A more melodic, meditative album, it features songs like "Little Wing", "If Six Was Nine", "Castles Made Of Sand", and "Spanish Castle Magic".

In Tin Pan Alley's tradition of expecting a fast pay-off from pop, *Axis: Bold As Love* is released before Christmas 1967, a rapid follow-up to *Are You Experienced?*; the record is an enormous seller, but cutting edge cultural parameters have overtaken the thinking of the men in the music business. As the concept of "rock" grows, albums become the central icons of the new underground; in interviews Jimi emphasises how his latest LP is designed to be listened to in stereo; along with their rivals Cream and Steve Winwood's new group Traffic, the Jimi Hendrix Experience is one of the first acts perceived by fans as specifically part of this newly dominant format.

By February 1968, the group is back in the United States, headlining arenas and theatres. *Are You Experienced?* has sold over a million copies there; and the newly released *Axis* is rising in the Top Twenty.

The Jimi Hendrix Experience are one of the biggest concert draws, and Jimi makes a triumphant return to Seattle when they play at the Center Arena on February 12. Al Hendrix is in the middle of the front row.

When the tour ends a few weeks later Hendrix virtually bases himself in New York. His restless creativity is becoming frustrated inside the rigid trio line-up of the Experience; he wants to play with other musicians, and pitch his ideas in other directions.

For Hendrix, of course, America is his home. For Redding and Mitchell it is but a place to tour and visit. At the height of its success, the winning formula behind the Jimi Hendrix Experience begins to dissipate.

Sessions for the new album are fixed at the Record Plant in New York. Although simply credited to the Jimi Hendrix Experience the eventual album, *Electric Ladyland*, also includes contributions from Jack Casady of Jefferson Airplane, Al Kooper, Buddy Miles and, from Traffic, Steve Winwood, Dave Mason and Chris Wood.

Hendrix, with Mitchell and Redding, spends much of the year travelling between Europe and the

United States, fulfilling a tortuous schedule of live dates and studio sessions. Jimi also takes plenty of time out to jam with other musicians: he plays a whole number of ad hoc club sessions with such bands and musicians as Electric Flag, Eric Clapton, Larry Coryell and Jeff Beck.

He also spends a considerable time with Buddy Miles, whom he has first met on an Isley Brothers/Wilson Pickett double-header some years before.

"All Along The Watchtower" is issued as a single on October 18, 1968. Although it is a Bob Dylan song, Hendrix's version is definitive; an epic interstellar performance which comes as the prelude to *Electric Ladyland*, released the following week.

This double album, recorded in both Britain and the United States, represents an extraordinary moment of creativity. It burns with energy, high on ambition and experiment. *Electric Ladyland* includes the near fifteen-minute groove of "Voodoo Chile" together with its five-minute little sister "Voodoo Child" (slight return). It also features "Crosstown Traffic", "Have You Ever Been (To Electric Ladyland)" and, of course, "All Along The Watchtower". *Electric Ladyland* establishes Hendrix as one of popular music's supreme artists. Not only is he the consummate guitarist of his age, but his unique approach to stage presentation and to music and lyric-writing seems truly from another world. The soundscapes he creates reflect his inner consciousness, itself a reflection of the totality of his experience in this and other lives.

Electric Ladyland gives Hendrix his only number 1 album in America and, despite the internal politics within the band, the Experience are nevertheless the top grossing act on the US concert circuit. The start of 1969, however, is spent in Britain and Europe. The Jimi Hendrix Experience give their last British performance at London's Royal Albert Hall on February 24.

Through all the changes, however, music remains Jimi's fundamental priority. Hendrix even sits in with the jazz great Roland Kirk at London's Ronnie Scott's Club; it is an indication of his increasing fascination with jazz.

Then comes the band's final American tour, ending at the Denver Pop Festival on June 29. Jimi's restless creativity, however, is consumed by new ambitions. At the height of the band's success its winning formula is feeling suffocating: the Experience implodes.

Home Coming (1968)

Shot backstage by Douglas Kent Hall on February 12 at the Center Arena, the first time that Jimi had been back to Seattle since his army days. The show was described by a local reviewer as being "rather subdued" - this possibly in deference to Jimi's family who occupied the centre of the front row. The day after, Jimi was supposed to be honoured with the Keys of the City of Seattle. However, since it was Lincoln's birthday, City Hall was closed so the ceremony never took place.

"Man, that Seattle thing was really something. The only keys I expected to see in that town were from the jailhouse. But I met my family and we were happy for a change. I told my dad, I could buy you a home. I want to buy you a home this winter. I've got a six-year-old sister, Janie, who I'd never seen. That is the time I've been gone. She's a lovely little girl. She keeps every article she reads about me and all the pictures. I've got a picture of her, she's so cute."

Doppelganger

(1967)

Jimi pictured by David Magnus outside Chas Chandler's flat in Montagu Square.
The premises were originally owned by Ringo Starr, and Jimi moved in with Kathy Etchingham during December 1966.

"I said I might as well go to England because nothing much was happening. We were making three dollars a night and starving! I only hope that the guys I left behind are doing all right. The way I left was kinda wrong - they all thought they were going. I've been in London three months but Britain is really groovy. I share a flat with Chas Chandler. It used to belong to Ringo. In fact, they only took the drums away the other day. There's stereo all over the place, a kinky bathroom and lots of mirrors. I want to stay in England and I understand there won't be any difficulty about getting work permits so long as I'm a good little boy!"

Photography : David Magnus / Rex Features

experienced?

October 1969: *OZ* editor Richard Neville smelled a hot, sexy story. Branded "groupies", a revolutionary species of woman was attracting shocked attention. Would I and Jenny Fabian, author of the hilarious novel *Groupie*, like to investigate for his magazine? When we were told he had arranged for us to interview Jimi Hendrix, we got going.

Hendrix! We had seen him on stage and off, squeezed past him many times down the Speakeasy where he would hang out for fun, a drink, a turn-on before returning to the recording studio.

I can remember getting carefully dressed for the occasion, surely more on my mind than merely interviewing Hendrix about what he thought of Women's Liberation. My hair back-combed, I chose my favourite crushed velvet dress. We never knew our luck, Jenny and I.

Lightheartedly we stood at the door of a darkened West End office. In the gloom we saw Hendrix lying back on a sofa surrounded by his entourage. Jenny walked up and politely introduced herself, and then she introduced me.

Leaping to his feet, Hendrix sprang forward as if to strike us.

"Coon!" he shouted, in a rage. "You call me a Coon! And your hair all frizzed up! How dare you come in here with frizzy hair an' call me a Coon. Get out! Get out!"

Before Jenny and I had time to explain, several burly minders had bundled us out into the street. That Jimi Hendrix thought we had purposefully insulted him was mortifying. His musicianship, let alone his beauty, filled us with awe. We felt lucky, honoured even, that, as an army grunt back in Kentucky, he had botched that parachute jump and chosen to land up in London. Flying through the air, Hendrix knew what it felt like. No wonder his songs with their slipstream tones and tumbling fluidity sound like nothing anyone had ever played before.

It was 1966, and Jimi Hendrix had arrived prepared, a fearless twenty-three-year-old with a notebook full of ideas for songs. As soon as he could, Hendrix asked us, "Are You Experienced?" He did want to know what we knew of the world, but entwined in his question was a widely understood innuendo. Experienced? In LOVE, of course!

Whether experienced in love or not, most of us understood there could be no better person to trust ourselves with, or learn from, than someone who had dived out of a C47 at 1,200 feet and survived the trip. That rush of letting go, of soaring, diving, in our own skins but out of it ... Hendrix would express his experience of these sensations in sound. For those who crave orgasmic ecstasy, the free-fall, here was Hendrix singing about flying over a love-filled sea, making love in the sky.

What made Hendrix fly high above an already outstanding group of musicians working in London "on the scene" was that he hadn't emerged from any scene. Instead, Hendrix emerged from a viciously segregated country where dance and musical expression were the essence of survival, the only amelioration of despair, the only way out.

Unlike white musicians who could choose music as a career, Jimi Hendrix had no freedom of choice. On June 10, 1970, from his cell in San Quentin prison, Black Power theorist and Soledad Brother George Jackson wrote: "Black men born in the US and fortunate to live past the

Art : Caroline Coon

Photograph : Ron Rafaelli / Michael Ochs Archives

age of eighteen are conditioned to accept the inevitability of prison. For most of us, it simply looms as the next phase in a sequence of humiliations." Racism, slavery, segregation, American apartheid – the kind of disaster which, unless you've experienced it, you can never understand. Within segregated America, so highly developed was the palliative of popular music, performance and showmanship, that from a black perspective, white popular culture, despite its power, was seen as inferior, ignorant, superficial and soulless.

White musicians on the scene in London, ignorant of the depth of racism in America and therefore limited in their understanding of Hendrix, were nevertheless galvanised by his arrival – as if he'd jumped from the sky in amongst them off another planet. Unlike stars such as Ike and Tina Turner, Ray Charles and Little Richard, Hendrix didn't arrive, perform and go home again. He stayed here, living and working, unavoidable, unnegotiable, putting imitators of black music into the greatest tizzy. Everyone – Alexis Korner, John Mayall, Long John Baldry, Mick Jagger, Pete Townshend, Eric Clapton – had to raise their game.

For Hendrix, London meant freedom from segregation and a calmer social and political atmosphere in which to elaborate his own skills, experiment with new recording techniques and develop a more complex way of playing. He began structuring his work as a process of sequential enquiry into his enduring motif – escape. Flying to freedom. He knew exactly what he wanted it to sound like.

Creativity and seriousness: this is the real Jimi Hendrix, a formidable musician on the cusp of new recording techniques and technology which he pushed to wild limits, creating a sound-world instantly recognisable as his own, and some of the most sacred songs in popular culture.

The Hendrix sound hits the spot, turns us on. That major/minor blur, redolent of classic blues and slavery, resolves into sounds that stand for well-being. We can't resist them. Often for technical reasons. Time and again, as in "Purple Haze" where Jimi and Noel harmonise the bass octaves in E with the guitars B flat plucked above, the Jimi Hendrix Experience delivers a welter of infamous tritones. (A tritone spans a 6h interval away from a keynote and the 6th harmonises with the most extreme dissonances relative to any other interval.) So potently erotic is a tritone that the medieval Church banned it as the "devil in music". Popular music is antithetical to orthodox church music. Celibate monks chant in order to subdue congregations into sexless, passive obedience, all the better to be controlled by Church and state. Popular music enlivens audiences and lures us beyond controls of Church and state by encouraging sexual pleasure, not to mention protest and revolution.

A rhapsodic outpouring of sexuality is integral to Hendrix's popular appeal. And inseparable from his sexuality is *discretion*. He would shrug off his sexual success, be a little apologetic and self-deprecating. In fact, for me to detail his sexuality might have offended him deeply. Quite apart from his good manners, for him to encourage an image of himself as overtly sexual was dangerous - literally life-threatening. Back in the USA in1966, beyond the segregation barrier, merely for a black man to look at a white woman was to risk getting shot, a political reality from which, even today, much "cool" and discretion is born.

At the very least Hendrix knew that people threatened by sex would use his sexuality out of its musicianship context to trivialise him. When the colour of your skin is a death sentence, and your sexuality demonised, to escape racist attack you become skilled at the cool art of making yourself seem invisible. Hence the paradox: in order to live among white people, some of the most beautifully sexy men on earth needed to downplay their sexuality, which made them even more sexually attractive. (By 1986, twenty years later, black hip hop musicians would boast and flaunt their sexuality, using hyper-masculinity as their strategy to combat racism.)

On stage Hendrix was as safe from prejudice as he'd ever be. Performing like a trapeze artist on a high wire, keeping a sophisticated balance between absolute discretion and ultimate display, Hendrix let fly. He became *sex*. Raunchy, the acme of *down*, he sang "make love, make love, make love …" projecting his feelings towards us as if on an infinite flow of come.

You could feel him getting to you, gentling you along for a while, letting you get glued into his mood. His voice, with its immaculate timing, was emotional and sincere. Confidently languid before self effacing Noel and Mitch, Hendrix tugged out unearthly, floating, slow, loose chords. He revealed his heart, the sad, dark side of his spirit. He knew all about anger and desperation, had no trouble expressing his feelings. But, he exhorted us, forget politics for a moment!

Then Hendrix lifted us into an ecstatic daze. Dancing, you could imagine making love to his music. His seductive performance presented itself as a site for the safe release of immemorial sensations of trance, worship, ritual. And on stage the Hendrix persona clarified, took on its most revolutionary aspect. His Fender Stratocaster weaving before him like a magic wand, he conjured up an ideal.

Like the *fuzz*-box blur of his music, Hendrix himself blurred the divide between masculine and feminine. On stage Hendrix confounded our expectations of what it was to be manly. On stage Hendrix seemed to change sex. His guitar, embodying the transformation, was thrust forward, stroked, nibbled, fondled, one moment a huge phallic extension, an erect, probing cock which Hendrix twirled around and sucked. And the next moment Hendrix seemed to unfold his guitar, open it out into a gleaming red female form, curvy, a cunt, which he went down on and licked. Blithely showing both how strong and delicate he could be, Hendrix was interchangeable, transerotic, an elision of man making love to woman, woman making love to woman, man making love to man. Hendrix's onstage shift into hermaphrodite mode was the first inkling many of us had of how far sexual liberation could go. Hendrix, his tongue extended, wet, licking his guitar into phallus and vagina shape is as hot an icon of *unisex* as you can see – a succinct expression of the sixties' peace and love desire for destructive polarities between the sexes to vanish, a prophetic indication of what was to come, a vivid lesson in adjustment to the future.

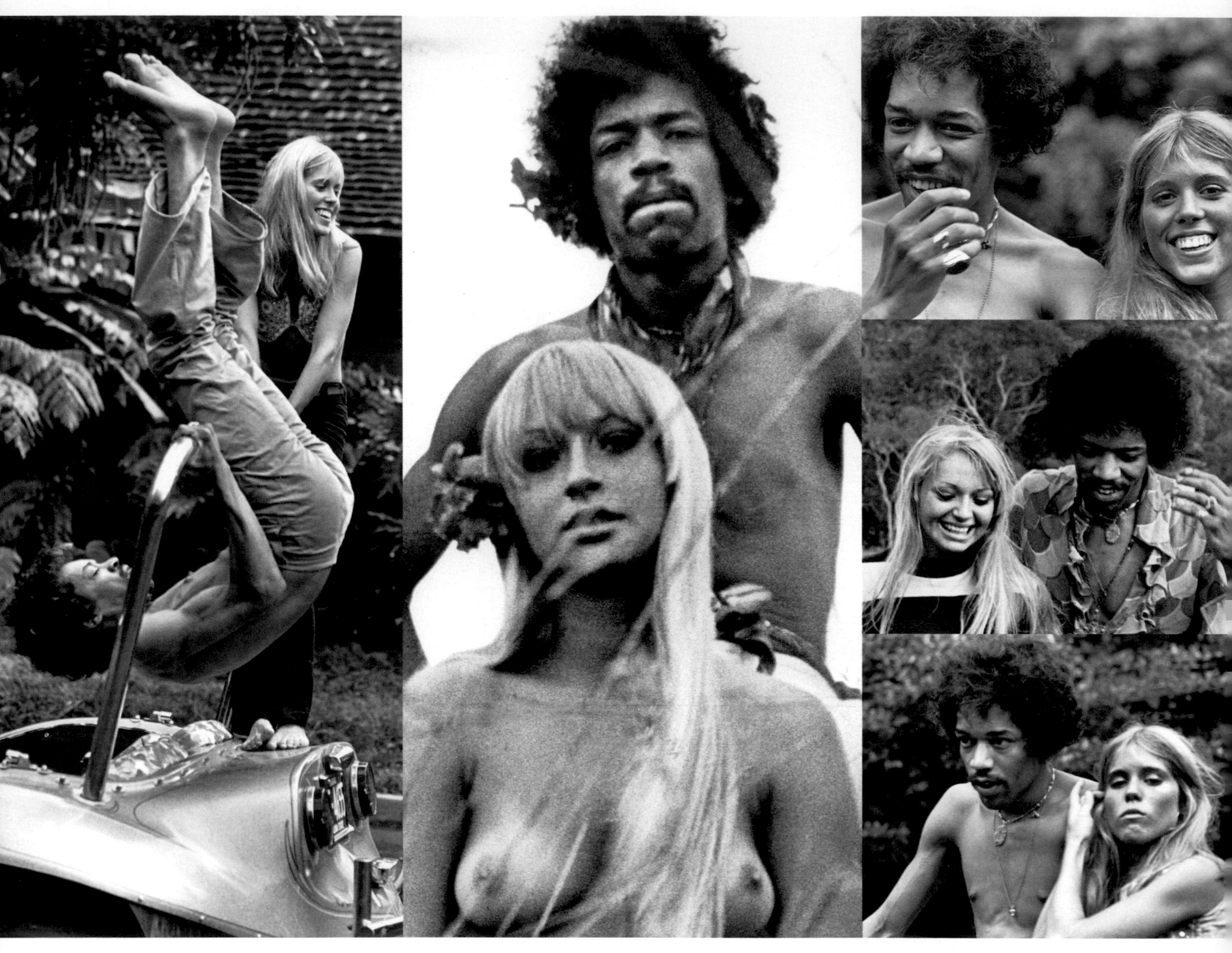

Photograph : Ron Rafaelli / Michael Ochs Archives

Chip technology, space travel, science fact, sexual revolution, gender dissolve: the twenty-first-century living experiment began. We struggled to free ourselves from war, heavy industry, pollution, class, race, sexual discrimination – and Hendrix was there creating the soundtrack. For a brief three years we believed we wouldn't have to work that hard for it. When Hendrix sang "I want to show you something new …" we innocently imagined the world would change overnight. Everything seemed possible, paradise even.

But hold on a minute! Didn't it all crash down to earth?

Yes, no sooner had musicians like Hendrix begun the sexual revolution than something horrible happened. Men in general discovered what women and homosexuals already knew. Blurring gender lines cause hysterical panic.

More than anything else, the sexual revolution rather than any anti-Vietnam marches provoked the police – goaded on by the press, politicians and the Church – to use drug laws in a ruthless attempt to eradicate the emergent pop culture. Like the Beatles, the Rolling Stones, Eric Clapton and thousands of us "hippies" who had been busted, often after having been planted with drugs, Jimi Hendrix was also arrested in suspicious circumstances.

By 1969 the clampdown was under way in earnest. The government spent millions of pounds banning free pop festivals, love-ins, *OZ* magazine. Many white pop stars got scared. Rich and successful, they could afford now to turn establishment. We watched in amazement as off stage they jumped into suits in order to become respectable enough to consort with royalty. What they wore on stage became an old-fashioned clownish drag, traditional joker's motley. When not cut off, their once significantly feminine long hair became macho, and the music Hendrix invented, that full-blown electric rock which was sensuous and lyrical when played by him, started to thrash into Heavy Metal.

Far from granting permission to both sexes, the late sixties turned exclusively male liberation, furiously anti-women, just like the established culture we hoped our peace and love movement would counteract. Men were out, upfront and often shockingly honest about their sexual needs and fantasies. Ninety-nine per cent of pop musicians said they were in groups to improve their pulling-power. Hendrix felt free to explain: "I need more woman than earth can hold by itself." Or, "And these girls are like one girl to me. Little Wing was a very sweet girl that came around and gave me her whole life/... and me with my crazy ass couldn't get it together, so I'm off here and off over there." When women sought similar sexual freedom to be off here and there they were called pejorative names.

Nothing is more indicative of pop culture's fearful retreat from sexual equality than the branding of sexually active women as *groupies*.

As men fled from gender blur in droves, women were rushing towards liberation, experiencing it to the hilt.

Prior to the sixties only men with power and money, the stage-door Johnnies, could indulge fantasies of getting close to beautiful stars. Now women, armed with the power of the pill and their own money, could experience the thrill of going to gigs, and backstage into the arms of pop gods. It was sport, hunting, going for

Art : Caroline Coon

what might be great sex, a response to the come-on, Hendrix singing, "I wanna show you, I wanna turn you on, I want you to be mine."

What must have horrified, shocked and threatened men most about women's sexual freedom was the extent to which it meant their own loss of power and control. Tables were turned. Foxy ladies were chasing the hounds.

It was a picture to behold, the look on a pop star's face when confronted by women brazen enough to mention their long lists of star conquests – which groupies often did – what a laugh! Two women, calling themselves the Plaster Casters, became famous for their collection of pop star erections, including that of Jimi Hendrix.

The phenomenal *experience* of these predatory, newly liberated women was both repelling and fascinating. "Female liberation movements are good news stories because of their atmosphere of perversion, female depravity, sensation and solemn absurdity," wrote Germaine Greer in the 1970 thrill *The Female Eunuch*. Nevertheless, she went on, "Nurses are misbehaving, teachers are on strike, skirts are all imaginable levels, bras are not being bought, abortions are being demanded ... rebellion is gathering steam and may yet become revolution."

When Richard Neville sent me and Jenny as *OZ* reporters to interview Jimi Hendrix about sexual equality, we could hardly have predicted the outcome. His explosive reaction to my name could only mean he was living on his nerves and subject to more racist attacks in London than we white people ever realised. At that time, calling black people "niggers", "coons", "wogs" was normal, commonplace. Before the 1968 Race Relations Act landlords boldly displayed signs proclaiming "No Irish, No Blacks, No Dogs" in their front windows. The first person to be arrested under the 1968 Race Relations Act, for making "racist" utterances against white people at Speakers' Corner, was Michael Abdul Malik, aka Michael X. Despite their supposed knowledge about other races, many people admitted that Jimi Hendrix was the first black person they had ever seen. For all his money and fame, for all the liberated women throwing themselves at his feet, away from home Jimi Hendrix must have been isolated and extremely lonely.

The last time I saw Hendrix he was on stage at the Isle of Wight Festival in 1970, worn down and dazed,

Photograph : Rancurel / Lampard

As you all know, you just can't believe everything you see and hear. Can you? Now, if you'll excuse me, I must be on my way.

Photograph : Michael Ochs Archives

falling with no parachute to save him this time. A few months after writing "Oh, give me some breath, give me some room to breathe, 'cause I don't necessarily want to breathe on you", he was dead, from inhalation of vomit after an overdose of sleeping pills – a tired accident. He was twenty-seven when he died, younger than Presley, Marley or Lennon.

No superlatives seem apt to describe the beauty and range of the sounds he left, one of the most powerful legends of suffering and transcendence in the popular culture of the twentieth century. Guts, grace, authentic emotion, experience, skill, call it what you like … Listening to Jimi Hendrix now, digging his oeuvre, you know he had it: he was the biggest cock of all – not like some Heavy Metal groups one could mention; for all their big noise, can we be sure they have any cock at all?

Caroline Coon
January 1995

Photograph : Rancurel / Lampard

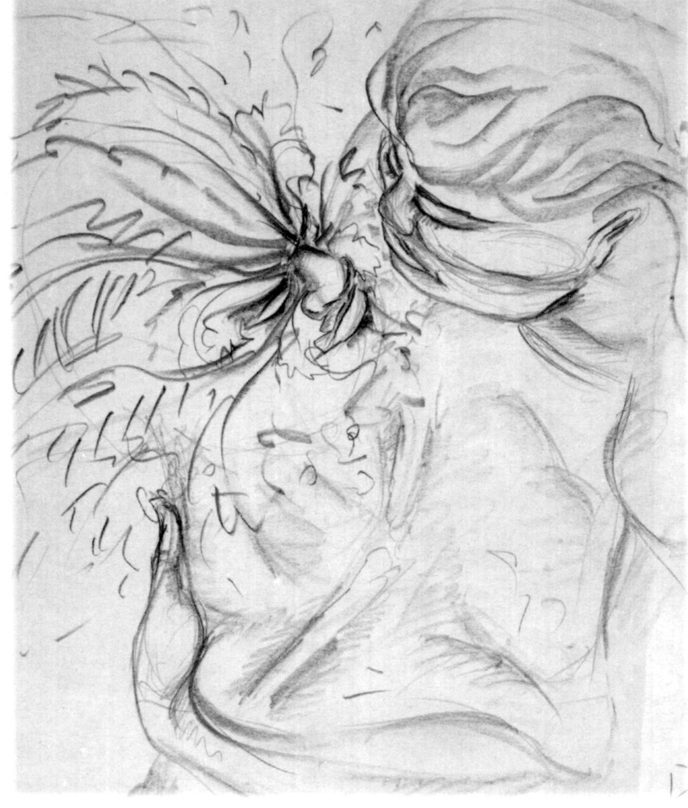

Art : Sue Young

"I was asked to make a video that expressed the essence of 'Fire', and I did it very much from the perspective of a female director. I was interested that Jimi was fascinated by the eternal inter-weaving of microcosmic and macrocosmic elements, by metamorphosis, the transformative energy flow. So I picked up on the theme of The Green Man and the notion of fertility, and tried to get a perspective that presented the idea of death and re-birth."

At Home (1967) Photograph : Terence Donovan

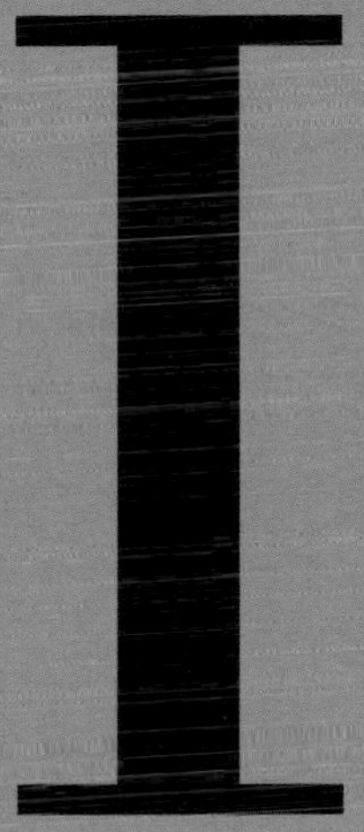

"I first saw Jimi in London at the Seven And A Half, a little club. Mick had seen him play in New York and said, 'He's going to tear the world apart.'

"He told me that Chas Chandler had come to him and taken him to see Jimi play in New York. He'd tried to get Mick to invest in him, but Mick saw what was coming and didn't want anything to do with it - it was as though he'd seen the future of music.

"The thing about him was that he was so sexual. He had that magnetic sexuality. And he was also very quiet. He didn't have to talk. It was almost like a scent he gave off. I didn't have an affair with him - it's my only lasting regret in life."

Marianne Faithfull

I just thought about the title. There might be a meaning behind the whole thing. The Axis of the earth turns around and changes the face of the world and completely different civilisations come about or another age comes about.

Electric Ladyland *is different to what we've ever done before. It wasn't just slopped together. Every little thing you hear on there means something... It starts with a ninety-second sound painting of the heavens. It's typifying what happens when the gods make love - or whatever they spend their time on.*

Why I'm kind of proud of Electric Ladyland *is that I really took the bulk of it through from beginning to end on my own, so that I can't deny it represents exactly what I was feeling at the time of production.*

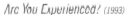

Are You Experienced? (1993)

Axis: Bold As Love (1993)

Electric Ladyland (1993)

"It's an awful cliché now, but Jimi really was terribly sweet. Very gentle, modest, quiet and unassuming. And pretty easy to work with, so long as you didn't actually ask him to do much. He knew he was Jimi and somehow, that was enough."

"I was shooting from very high up and very close in to him. But Jimi, being Jimi, was pretty stoned and kept on rocking back and forth. I had to say to him. 'Stand still, you keep on going in and out of focus!' He didn't smile a lot. It's not that he didn't normally, just that he didn't turn it on in a false way for the camera. Contrived? No way, Jimi was just Jimi, he didn't know how to be contrived."
GERED MANKOWITZ

From black and white originals, shot by Gered Mankowitz at his Mason's Yard studio in 1967.

Photograph / Art : Gered Mankowitz and David Costa

He was like a Venusian, like someone from another planet. All that hair. And there were hardly any black people in Newcastle - I think he actually was the first black person I'd ever seen. It was absolutely electric, almost too awesome to deal with. You felt like you were on the edge of a precipice. "Hey Joe" had come out only the week before. That was what decided me to become a musician, although I'd probably decided in some vague way already. But seeing a live gig like that was so much more effective than listening to records. I'd been into the Beatles before, but this was the beginning of rock music as opposed to rock 'n' roll. It was heavy.

Sting

T WAS H AVY

Photograph / Art : Gered Mankowitz and David Costa

James Marshall Hendrix *(1967)*

Photograph : Dezo Hoffman

The Gallery Screen Print (1992)
"Me, the world's greatest? That's silly."

PSIKHODELIK

Contrary to popular belief and geopolitical logic, the Soviet rock community in the sixties wasn't hopelessly backward and isolated from progressive trends. I personally first heard Jimi Hendrix on the radio as early as late 1966 ("Hey Joe", indeed) – and so did many thousands of Russian rock fans, as stations like BBC World Service and Russian service, Voice of America, Radio Luxembourg and even obscure ones like Radio Sweden or Radio Liberty in Polish or Romanian were religiously listened to.

In the particular case of Hendrix, the information was not only smuggled through capitalist propaganda airwaves, but also much hyped in the local communist press. Always eager to display the sickness and absurdity of the Western way of life and the decadence of its culture, Soviet "counter-propaganda" immediately seized upon the Monterey Festival story of Jimi burning his guitar and promoted juicy pictures with typical comments which read like: "The notorious 'big beat' vandals didn't get enough when they smashed their guitars onstage. Now they've brought their musical hooliganism to a further degree: at a festival in California one of the so-called 'artists' has burned his instrument during the performance, cheered on by a drug-soaked crowd."

Another description of that same Monterey performance claimed to unearth a more sinister motivation: "The bosses of Western showbusiness force their marionette artists to do the most stupid and disgusting tricks for the sake of publicity. Recently one of the newest pop heroes, playing in front of a huge audience, has licked his electric guitar, pretending that he's eating it, and later setting it on fire. It's not excluded, that in an attempt to create more noise around themselves, Western pop idols will start to mutilate their own bodies." (Iggy Pop was yet to arrive ...) Jimi's name was always misspelled in the 'correct' way, as Jimmy.

By the end of the sixties, Jimi Hendrix was considered the musical/spiritual leader of the Soviet rock community. Gone was Beatlemania and harmony vocals; now at the top of the Soviet dissident music agenda there was something called "Psikhodelik"- a word for which very few knew the exact translation, but everyone understood that it meant something like "far out" and "freak out". Jim Morrison was the voice of this new movement, but Jimi definitely personified its sound.

An interesting issue is that no one in the Soviet Union associated Hendrix and his music with the black r&b tradition and the likes of James Brown, Wilson Pickett or even Sly Stone. He, just like Frank Zappa or Pink Floyd, was seen as an avant-garde musician rather than radical bluesman. Probably this has happened thanks to the monumental popularity of Electric Ladyland album – which, by the way, was by far the most expensive Western LP on the black market (in original sleeve, no bullshit), costing there more than an average monthly wage (120 roubles or, at the then illegal exchange rate, $50). Jimi was also responsible for the emergence of a new home-based industry – the local manufacturing of wah-wah pedals.

Impossible to date accurately, this archival record company publicity still, with Jimi striking a very Leninist pose was probably taken early to mid-1967.

Sure enough, this morning came unto me
Silver wings silhouette against the child's sunrise
And my Angel, she said unto me
Today is the day for you to rise

JIMI HENDRIX IN THE SOVIET UNION

Art Troitsky : February/March 1995

I first heard about Jimi Hendrix's death on a heavily jammed Voice of America news programme. The Soviet press didn't show much response at all; I only remember a nastily ironic piece about a desperate girl fan who threw herself out of a window, crying "I'm coming to you Jimi!", after learning that he had died. But there was much more one month later, when Janis Joplin followed Jimi to heaven: now the Soviet media could label these deaths as another deadly decadent trend in capitalist society (which, in a way, it was ...). "More pop idols burn themselves on an altar of showbusiness," ran a headline in one newspaper. Both Jimi and Janis were described with a degree of sympathy like lost souls, manipulated and squeezed out by the ruthless "system".

Long after 1970 Jimi Hendrix's legacy lived on in Russia. Many bands played cover versions of his songs, "Purple Haze" and "Voodoo Chile" being the two most popular numbers. Some groups, in fact, created their entire repertoire out of Jimi's music. Moscow's Second Wind was the most famous among Hendrix copycats. Second Wind's singer/guitarist Igor Degtiariuk was self-proclaimed and widely known as the "Russian Jimi Hendrix": he copied Jimi's style in everything, including the most incredible tapestry-made flares in town, an Afro hairdo and wild sexual behaviour. Just like Jimi, he too went too far with drugs, was arrested for possession and spent some time in a jail-type psychiatric clinic. Right now, he's alive and relatively well, bald headed and working in a TV archive. He still occasionally performs with his band. "Jimi Hendrix has been my first and major influence," says Degtiariuk, "and it was the right influence. You know, in the mid-seventies I started to play music that was trendy then – all this jazz-rock, Mahavishnu stuff, and so on ... But this was a passing stage. The music that has remained with me, the music that I play now is the Hendrix-inspired blues. Because if in music you're looking for such a quality as freedom, you should look no further than Jimi Hendrix."

Courtesy : Caesar Glebbeek Collection

Photograph : Michael Ochs Archives

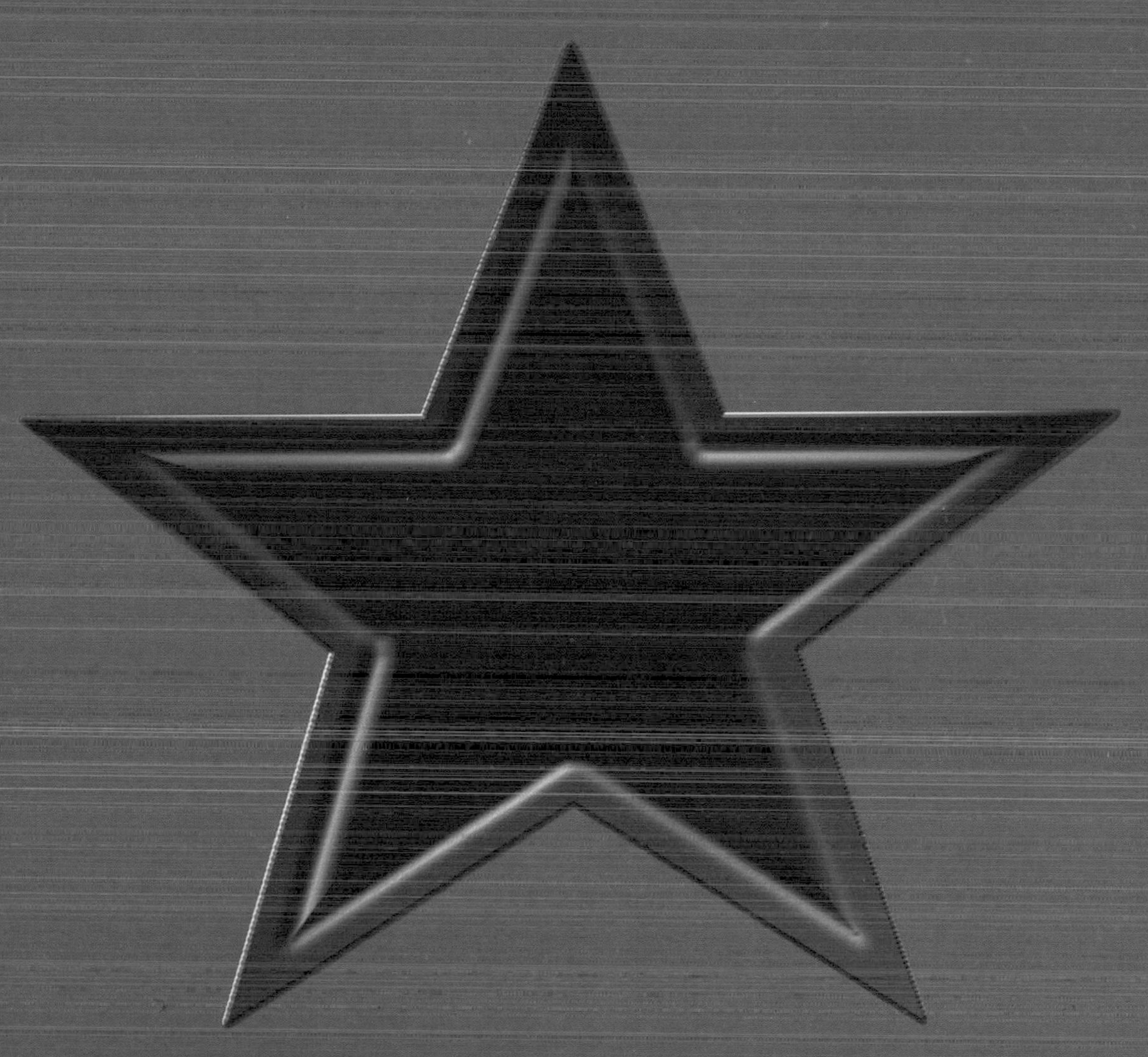

JIMI HENDRIX

Re-Wired (1992)

"Honestly, I don't know why the people want to see me as a horror-type. They'd love it if I looked like a cannibal."

Ian Wright's view of Jimi was inspired, initially, by the work of Martin Sharp, most especially by his sixties poster of Dylan, *Mr Tambourine Man*. This started life as a hand-drawn and computerised image which was then, variously, Xeroxed on to coloured paper. By degrees, the portrait began almost to assemble itself, layer upon layer, as the coloured pages were torn apart and stuck back together again with judicious use of Gel Medium.

Art : Ian Wright

Photograph : Robert Knight

You jump in front of my car
When you know all the time
That ninety miles an hour girl
is the speed I drive
You tell me it's alright
You don't mind a little pain
You say you just want me to take you for a drive
You're just like Crosstown traffic
So hard to get through to you
I'm not the only soul who's accused of hit and run
The tracks all across your back
I can see you had your fun
But darlin' can't you see
My signals turn from green to red
And with you I can see a traffic jam straight up ahead
I don't need to run over you
All you do is slow me down
(Crosstown Traffic)

Photography : Linda McCartney

Photography : Jean-Pierre Leloir

Photograph : Ron Rafaelli / Michael Ochs Archives

Composure (1968)

Most probably shot in the house Jimi had rented in Benedict Canyon, Los Angeles, during a short October holiday away from the madding crowd. Jimi's main hang-out during this break in touring was a club named in his honour, Thee [sic] Experience. He played there every night for a week, ending up running up a bar bill in excess of $1,000. The cash kept the club afloat.

"This is the drag about being on tour constantly, we never get to see the places we play. I am very tired. Not physically, just mentally. I haven't had time off since I've been in this scene. When you first make it the demands on you are very great. For some people they are just too heavy."

Electric Religion.

When I get up on stage and sing, that's my whole life - that's my religion. I am Electric Religion.

Photograph : Jean-Pierre Leloir

Talk About Me Like A Dog
Talk About the Clothes I Wear
But they don't realise they're the ones who're square

LORD KITCHENER'S VALET

by NEIL SPENCER

Jimi wore it like he talked it and played it: loud, wild and entirely individual.

At a time when black chic meant the buttoned-up, razor-smooth mohairs of the soul world that had just spat him out, Hendrix invented the templates for black hippie and black rocker virtually single-handed. In doing so, he assured himself a place in pop iconography that's proved as enduring and influential as his music.

The major spur for Jimi's sartorial evolution was the trend-conscious London scene into which he plunged in 1966. He co-opted the regency ruffles and velvets of London's rock aristocracy as effortlessly as he took over its clubs and girlfriends, bringing a tousled insouciance to the prevailing foppish look that was equalled only by the studiedly dishevelled Keith Richards and the inventive Brian Jones. On Jimi, no item of clothing was ever fully fastened, everything, except the loin-hugging trousers, was worn loose and free.

Aside from the bold features and fashionably whip-slim physique (and the fact he was black), it was Hendrix's processed, electric halo of hair that was the most shocking stylistic statement of his first London days. No one had ever seen anything like it (Jimi may have been inspired by Bob Dylan's Highway 61 look). Here was the visual equivalent of the freedom and imagination Jimi brought to his playing and performance. Without the hair, and the artfully unbuttoned look that went with it, the "wild man" would have appeared considerably tamer. Jimi's other early trademark was his Victorian military jacket, already a chic item on the London "underground" scene, and championed by the likes of the Beatles and arch-face Eric Clapton. It was Hendrix, though, for whom it became a signature garment. He bought two early in '67; the first almost austere, and quickly encrusted with a Jimi brooch, the second a

Photography : Michael Ochs Archives

Photograph : David Magnus / Rex Features

flamboyant black and gold affair which Jimi used to fantasise had once been worn in battle, and which he was disappointed to discover was in fact the dress jacket of a veterinary officer in the Crimea.

Jimi also favoured a Victorian cape for a while (see the cover of *Are You Experienced?*), another item unearthed from the imperial attic by enterprising retailers like Portobello Road's I Was Lord Kitchener's Valet. Hendrix brought a dazzling incongruity to Kitchener chic. With their mutton-chop sideburns, droopy moustaches and flowing hair, English rock stars were effectively spoofing the Victorian officer class whose finery they donned. But a grinning, crazy-haired Hendrix in hussar's jacket suggested something else entirely – a redskin brave showing off the spoils of a paleface scalp, perhaps, or a negro "buffalo soldier" fighting on the side of the anti-slavery Yankee forces in the US Civil War.

Jimi embraced other aspects of the London underground look: elephant-collared silk and satin shirts in cosmic swirls and acid-fried colours; knotted paisley scarves; velvet trousers; chunky eastern jewellery. A particular favourite was the black velvet waistcoat trimmed with gold braid that he wears on the cover of *Are You Experienced?*, and which crops up repeatedly in photographs over the next couple of years.

Not that Jimi ever considered himself a fashion plate. A natural extrovert, he wore what he pleased, rarely bothering to distinguish between his onstage and offstage appearance. No matter how outlandish the garb, there's Jimi in some scuzzy Hamburg bar in exactly the same thing he'd worn on stage a few hours previously. Hanging out at rehearsals or studio, he'd still be dressed like a rock regent.

It would be a mistake to think that Hendrix had no style of his own prior to his encounter with Carnaby Street. During his years working on the soul circuit – what he later described as "the Top 40 Soul R&B Hit Parade package with the patent leather shoes and hairstyle combined" – he was repeatedly in trouble for failing to conform to the exacting dress codes of the era. Bobby Womack recalls the young Jimi as "raggedy – all his clothes looked like they came from a rummage sale", while King Curtis reportedly sacked his wayward guitarist for refusing to wear regulation tie and cufflinks.

Little Richard, too, was driven to distraction, not only by Hendrix's hatred of band uniforms, but by the fact that he, the king of rock and rhythm, was being upstaged. "I'm the one who's going to look pretty on stage," declared Richard, who later claimed, probably justly, that Hendrix borrowed aspects of his image, notably Richard's pencil moustache and headband. Jimi's stay in New York had also left its hipster mark. Black proto-hippie Arthur Lee, with whom Hendrix was friendly in 1965, around the time Lee formed his West Coast band Love, may also have been an influence on Jimi's dress sense.

In any case, San Franciscan chic left its mark when Jimi played the Monterey Festival and other US dates in the summer of '67. Afghan waistcoats, fringed moccasin boots, emerald green trousers and copious amounts of Native American jewellery made their appearance in his wardrobe. So did a gold link belt slung over his hips and several oversized pendants; in fact, with his casually undone shirts, necklaces and totems, Jimi could be claimed as one of the origins of the seventies medallion man, the sensual stud.

That summer also saw Jimi acquire a "natural", the unprocessed hairstyle ushered in by black pride, though Jimi's cut never turned into the symmetrical "Afro" sported by black icons like Sly Stone and Angela Davis. His moustache also grew fuller.

Thereafter, in common with almost every other pop star of the era, Hendrix bloomed ever more colourfully. The military jacket gave way to flowery monstrosities (a green and pink floral affair, which he wore for the cover of *Axis: Bold As Love*, was a favourite), while the shirts likewise became ever more rainbow-hued and droopy-sleeved.

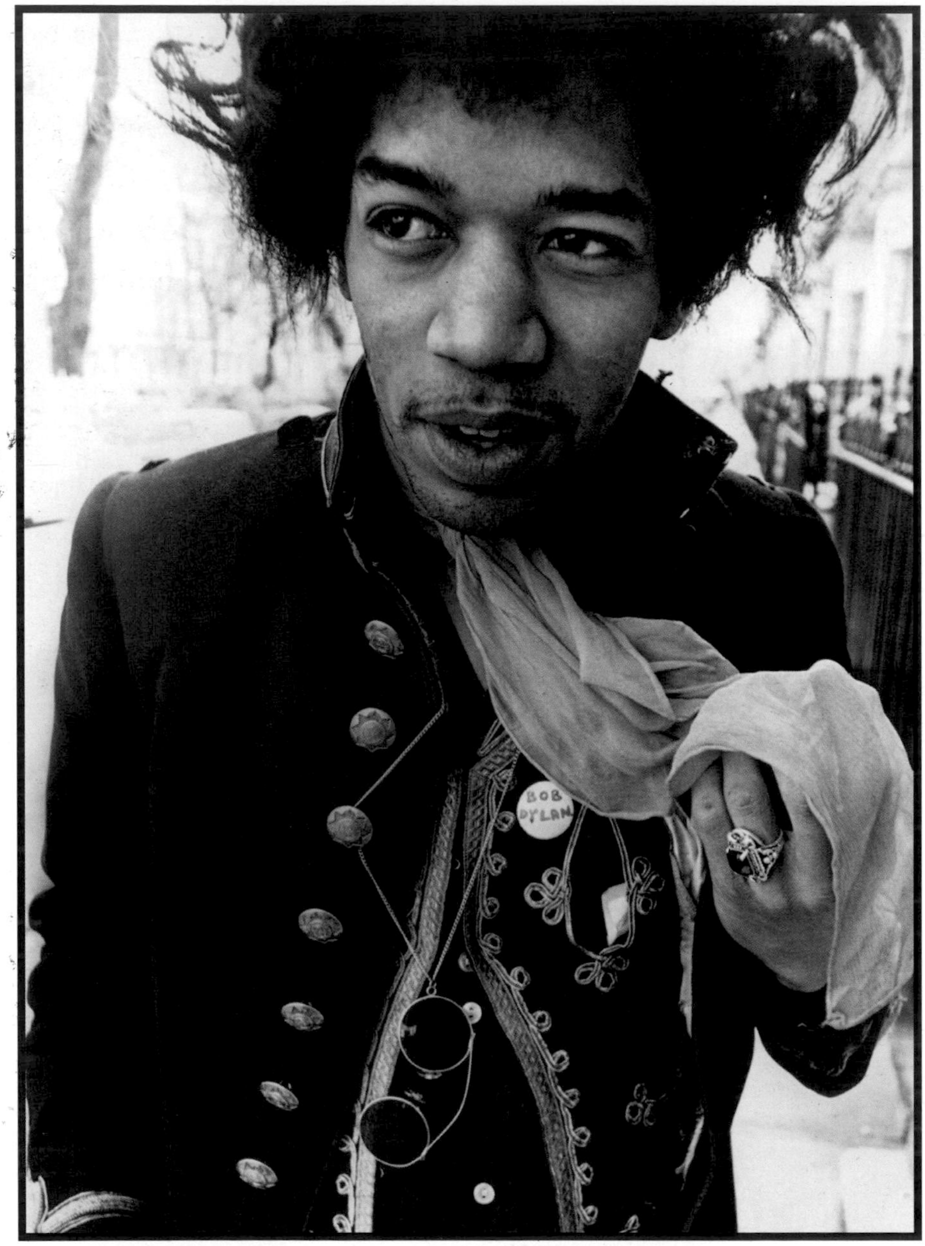

Photograph : David Magnus / Rex Features

While Jimi displayed hippie peacock finery at its most ornate and multi-layered, he offset the look with the black domed hat that became another trademark feature, and without which he was rarely seen for a year or two. Such hats, usually in pastel shades, were part of the emergent "pimp" look which black music would adopt in the seventies, but the way Jimi wore his, decorated with sun brooches and feathers, carried other codes. Here was Jimi the gypsy, the itinerant soothsayer and Voodoo Chile, peering mysteriously from beneath a black brim.

The alternative to the hat was the headband, a knotted paisley bandanna, borrowed from American hippies, which by the time of his celebrated Woodstock appearance in '69 had become another Hendrix signature. Woodstock marked the high point of hippie utopianism in dress as well as ideals. Jimi never dressed more extravagantly than at Woodstock, with his giant loon pants and his white buckskin jacket with foot-long fringes (a creation that, while rooted in the US frontier, was adorned with Native American designs). Thereafter he reverted to what was, for him, comparative restraint, though he continued to favour outlandish colours – magenta, chartreuse and purple were dominant – and floral patterns for the rest of his life. No one dressed, or played, noisier than Jimi.

Jimi's look has been massively influential in pop's subsequent history. As a black rocker he has been a lodestar for the likes of Carlos Santana, Phil Lynott, Prince, Vernon Reid and Lennie Kravitz, who have all dipped into his wardrobe. In the case of Prince, with his pencil moustache, his satin jackets, ruffled shirts, and matador pants, not to mention his oral guitar play, the debt is clearly immense, though Little Richard, too, deserves some credit here.

Post-Hendrix, the bandanna'd guitarist – a man on a serious quest is the implication, by association with both Indian braves and Vietnam soldiers – has become a cliché.

The headgear of Mark Knopfler, the Edge, Bruce Springsteen and countless others can be traced back to Jimi's trail-blazing axeman poses. Even Keith Richards, who passed his own brand of dishevelled, wasted chic on to scores of lesser rock gods, probably owes Jimi a scarf or two knotted around the thigh. Then there's "new romantic" Adam Ant, flogged a job lot of second-hand Hendrixalia by Malcolm McLaren for his Prince Charming act; what, after all, were Adam's hussar jacket, leg scarves and Red Indian trappings but Jimi's cast-offs?

In his sartorial style, as in the rest of his life, Hendrix was his own man. He could carry a suit as coolly as he wore a kimono – there was a jade green two-piece and the reefer-jacketed pin-stripe he wore for his drugs trial in late '69 – but there were certain rules even he adhered to. Once he left the soul circuit, he seems never to have worn a tie again. He never wore T-shirts, and he almost never wore jeans. If not necessarily stoned, Jimi was always beautiful.

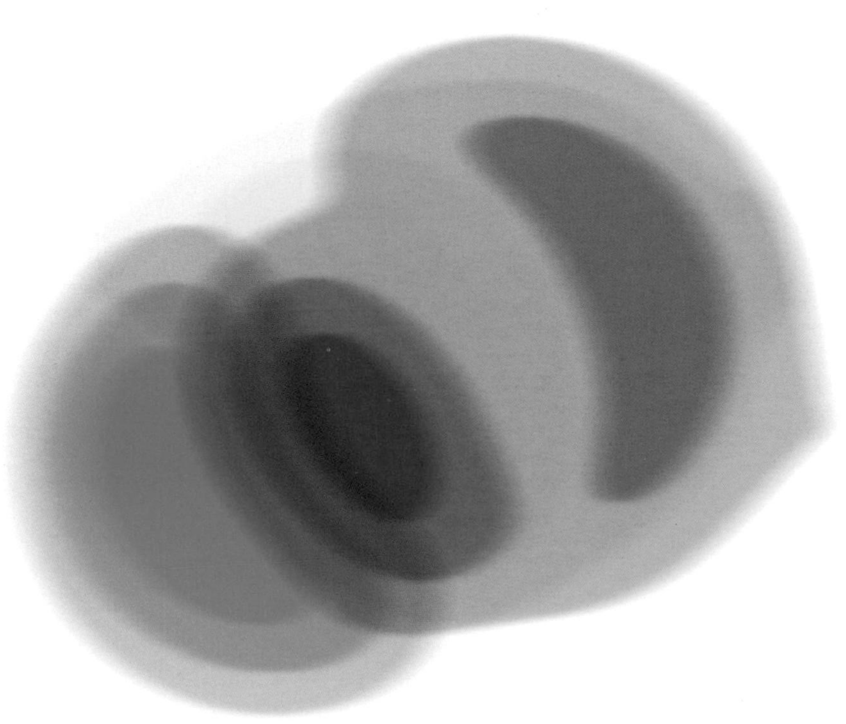

Royal Albert Hall. London November 14, 1967.
Photograph : Val Wilmer.

Farewell to the fun at the funfair : Jimi at the Isle of Wight

It was way past midnight, cold and misty, with searchlights criss-crossing the crumpled crowd. Roadies scurried across the stage, making final adjustments to the sound system, piling up extra amplification. There was an expectant hush. A familiar figure shambled on stage. A little burst came from the guitar, people sat up. Silence. The tangle-head mumbled apologies, looking confused and frustrated. His fingers rattled again across the strings. "Hell, I just ain't came," Jimi Hendrix muttered. It was sad and eerily moving. People were crying. I saw flames lick at his frizz, but it was a trick of the lighting. "Hell, I just ain't came yet . . . "

Charles Shaar Murray, the older-than-his-years know-all Oz schoolkid, rushed up and shook my shoulders. He was raving, tears streaming down his cheeks. "The end, the end . . . we've come to the end," he wept. "It's all over now. Gone, gone . . ." Yes, baby blue, I felt it too. Farewell to the joy of the Jimi Hendrix Experience, farewell to the fun at the funfair. "Everything I ever believed in is kaput. Jimi failed because we all failed. We gouge each other's faces with Coke cans – we've created nothing, nothing . . ." Charles melted away into the darkness.

By now thousands in the audience were holding up torches and candles. Hendrix finally found his fuse and erupted: "Hey Joe, where you goin' with that gun in your hand?"

There was Azula dancing with a long silk scarf, over by the battery of speakers. Smoke rose from the stage. "We seem to have a fire," called out the MC, his voice tense. "Can someone help?" A drinking-water truck pulled up as I reached the side of the stage. The crew fiddled with inadequate hoses. But the source of the smoke was a ship's distress flare, swiftly extinguished. A voice muttered: "Fuckin' Mick Farren."

By Richard Neville

I'd never been to England before. I said I might as well go because that's the way I live my life... I could play louder over there - I could really get myself together over there. There wasn't so many hang-ups as there was in America, you know, mental hang-ups and things like that.

My music isn't pop. It's ME. That's why I like us being called the Experience. It's right... If it must be a tag I'd like it to be called Free Feeling. It's a mixture of rock, freak out, blues and rave music. My rock blues funky freaky sound.

We all dug "Hey Joe" as a number... Timmy Rose was the first to do it slowly. I like it played slowly... It was the first time I ever tried to sing on a record.

The Beatles used to come and see us sometimes, like at the Saville Theatre, and Paul McCartney told me they were planning to do a film and he wanted us to be in this film. We weren't known then and McCartney was trying to help us.

The world is getting to be a drag. What I hate is this thing of society these days trying to put everything and everybody into little tight cellophane compartments. I hate to be in any kind of compartment unless I choose it myself.

Photograph : Jean-Pierre Leloir

I just got tired, man, I just couldn't stand it anymore. I can't tell you the number of times it hurt me to play the same notes, the same beat. I was just a kind of shadowy figure up there, out of sight of the real meaning. I wanted my own scene, making my own music. I had these ideas and sounds in my brain, but I needed people to do it with and they were hard to find.

I just got tired, man, I just couldn't stand it anymore. I can't tell you the number of times it hurt me to play the same notes, the same beat. I was just a kind of shadowy figure up there, out of sight of the real meaning. I wanted my own scene, making my own music. I had these ideas and sounds in my brain, but I needed people to do it with and they were hard to find.

I just got tired, man, I just couldn't stand it anymore. I can't tell you the number of times it hurt me to play the same notes, the same beat. I was just a kind of shadowy figure up there, out of sight of the real meaning. I wanted my own scene, making my own music. I had these ideas and sounds in my brain, but I needed people to do it with and they were hard to find.

I just got tired, man, I just couldn't stand it anymore. I can't tell you the number of times it hurt me to play the same notes, the same beat. I was just a kind of shadowy figure up there, out of sight of the real meaning. I wanted my own scene, making my own music. I had these ideas and sounds in my brain, but I needed people to do it with and they were hard to find.

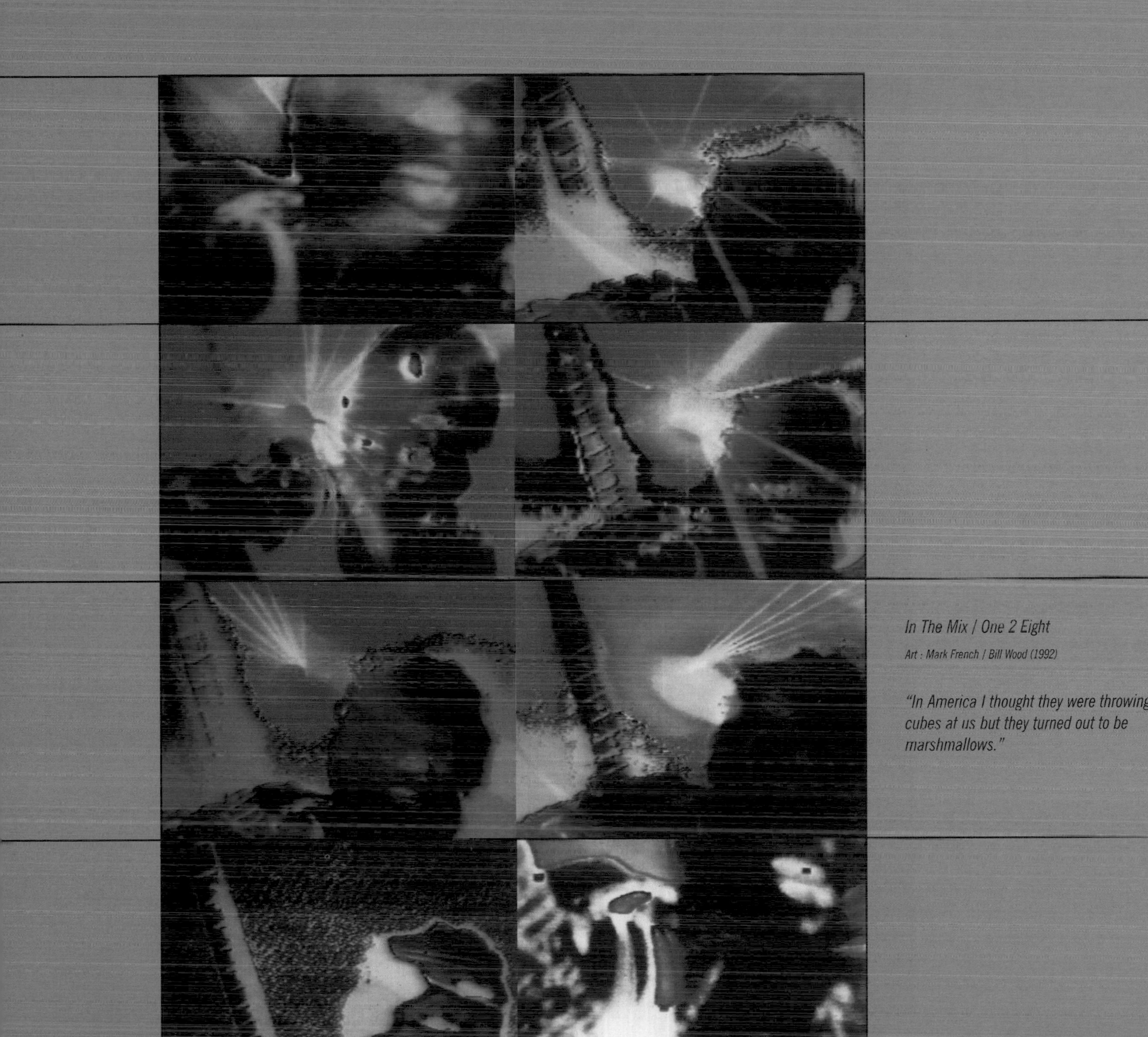

In The Mix / One 2 Eight

Art : Mark French / Bill Wood (1992)

"In America I thought they were throwing sugar cubes at us but they turned out to be marshmallows."

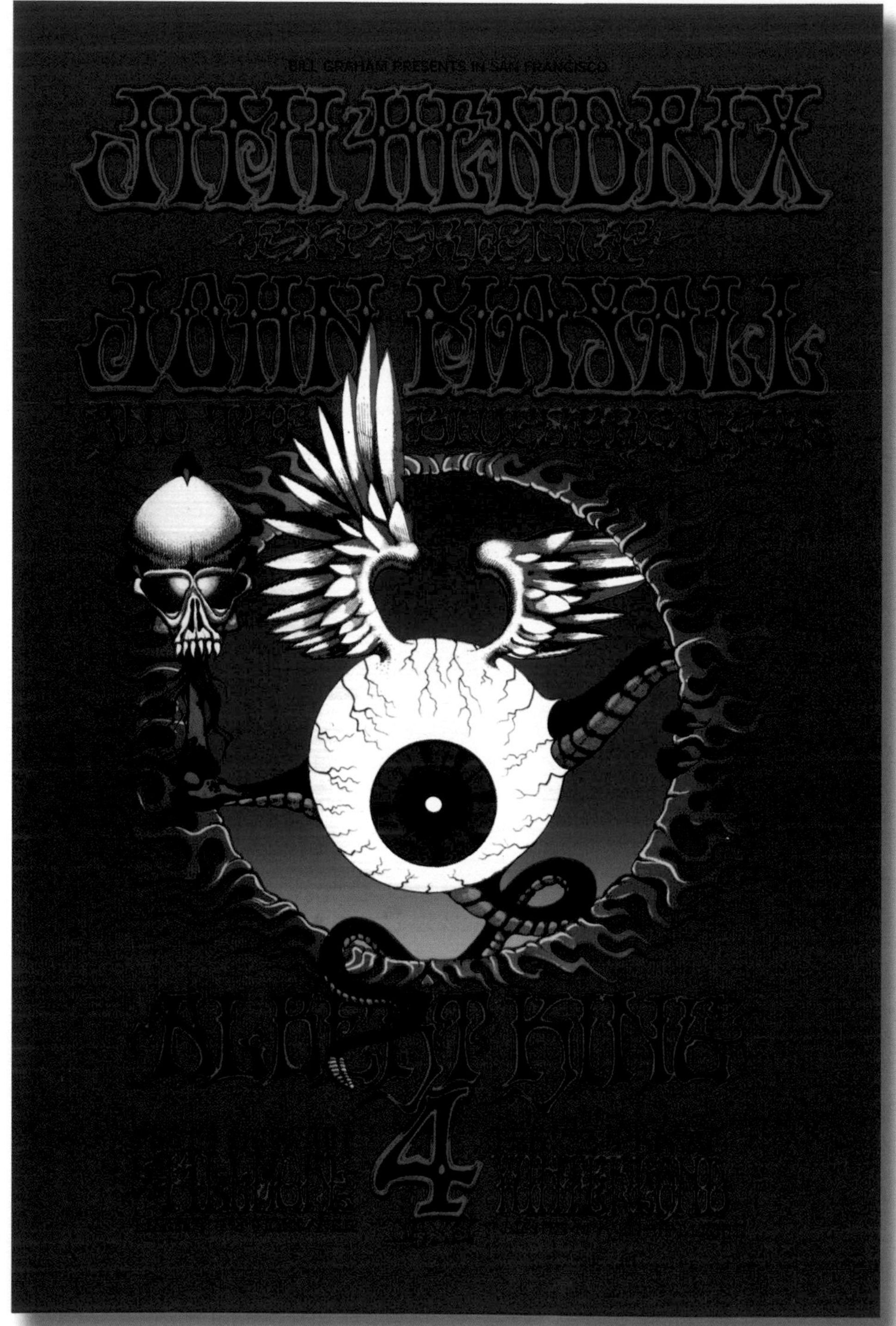

The Eyeball (1968)
Art : Rick Griffin / BGP Archives

The legendary Rick Griffin is recognised by many as the leading exponent of poster art over the past twenty-five years, his work being characterised by a richness of imagery that always contained multiple meanings. Griffin's New York Times *obituary described his masterpiece,* The Eyeball, *as one of the finest examples of this genre of art. Dating from February 1968, this poster was worked up for one show at San Francisco's Fillmore West auditorium and three at Winterland. Show tickets, all with the same design as the poster, alternated colour each night to enable the doormen at the venues to determine that ticket holders had the correct accreditation.*

'MONTEREY' & 'BEATLES' & OTHER PASSWORDS

I met Jimi Hendrix once and I saw him perform once. These occasions didn't coincide and each was long ago and far away and very pleasant to remember.

I first heard his name in April 1967 when Paul McCartney and Mal Evans were staying with Joan and me and the children in the house we had on Kirkwood, off Laurel Canyon in Los Angeles when hope was new and our world was full of colour and anticipation. Good times were here to stay if you were bathed in psychedelia.

Paul was invited that week to be one of the thirteen "governors" of the Monterey Pop Festival of which somehow I was a founder. The idea of governors was that they were men of distinction with a contribution to make. Paul's role was as an encourager. He told one of the producers, John Phillips of the Mamas and Papas, that his best suggestion, off the top of his head, was that the festival should "definitely include Jimi Hendrix" – because he was "great".

("Great" was quite a word then. It had replaced "fab", would be ousted by "fantastic" which in turn has given way to "brilliant", I notice.)

Jimi Hendrix was not well known in LA. A visitor to the festival offices at 8424 Sunset Boulevard in Hollywood was hanging out in my room, feet up on desk, smiling broadly from the effects of morning reefer, and wanting to know what was what and who was who, this fine day.

He (un-named for this little piece) was already hooked and booked for the festival, a "must" act because of his seminal status in the mid-sixties LA "scene". I told him Paul was in town, was now a governor and had suggested Jimi Hendrix for the festival. "Oh, Jesus... not that guy!"

"Oh?"

"He's just about an OK guitarist out of Seattle and he had to go to England to make any

Art : Rick Griffin / BGP Archives

noise which he has done, with some party tricks."

"So . . . not so good, huh?"

"OK if you like a guy who plays guitar with his teeth or behind his back or up his fuckin' ass."

Quite a CV in the time of music, love, flowers and peace.

John Phillips and his fellow producer Lou Adler nonetheless heeded their fellow governor and called Chas Chandler and Jimi was in.

The festival leaflet, printed some weeks ahead of the three-day event, shows Hendrix on the bill for the first night. The list runs: the Association, the Buffalo Springfield, the Grateful Dead, Jimi Hendrix, Laura Nyro, Lou Rawls, and Simon and Garfunkel.

In fact, though most of that list did perform on the first night, Jimi Hendrix was switched to Sunday night and it placed him on the same bill as the Who with whom (the archives show) he had appeared in London in January 1967 at a concert attended by the Beatles and other pop royalty when such things mattered and were not – imagine! – even sneered at.

Hendrix, by the time he set the festival ablaze on that Sunday night in June 1967, had acceptance at every level in England – including real street cred, though that phrase hadn't been coined, let alone overused. His commercial success would follow his triumph at Monterey. Mo Ostin and Joe Smith of Warner-Reprise were among dozens of record company "signers" in the audience.

He was just terrific. I won't throw adjectives around. He looked and

The Beetle *(1968)*
Art : Rick Griffin and Victor Moscoso
BGP Archives

A complex combination of Griffin and Moscoso's styles provided the art for this poster which was created for a three-night run at San Francisco's Winterland in October '68. The original poster was peculiarly sized - in order for it to be placed on telegraph poles. The Beetle, which in this instance uses Griffin's lettering, amply illustrates the influence of their comic book art and is a rare example of their collaborative work. The insect is a scarab, considered to be sacred by the Ancient Egyptians.

The Medusa Head *(1969)*

Art : Professor Gunther Kieser

Professor Gunther Kieser's extraordinary image of Jimi as a latter-day Medusa was originally created for a German tour and is widely considered to be one of the finest examples of rock art ever created. Indeed, Professor Kieser has been hailed by such an august body as the Museum Of Modern Art in New York as one of the greatest poster artists of all time. The snakes that were the Greek's hair have been updated to multicoloured wires and the design seeks to evoke the electricity of Jimi's music (note the on/off switch!) Gunther Kieser's poster also underwent one of the most complex printing processes possible: the separations were layered one on top of the other using transparent ink - similar to a watercolour glazing technique. To compensate for the limitations of colour technology, Touchplates - made from a combination of existing filmwork and airbrushing - customised the colours in order to bring the print to an exact colour and textural reproduction of the original art.

performed like an established star, with confidence, subtlety and his brilliance and his kneeling and chuckling and crouching and general weirdness with the lighter fuel (which could have misfired in any sense of the word) were a great coup and could only have been followed by the Who who also took a status leap on that show.

It was quite a night and though the Mamas and Papas (who closed) had a million hit singles, it was Jimi's performance which survived the years and is an indelible pop "icon" moment. All that fire, all those feathers! Not to mention "Wild thing ... I think ... I love ya." In the words of Sid Field: "What a performance."

By the time the festival was over and Hendrix's success sealed, my friend, his detractor, was quiet on the subject. "Did I say that?"

It was Hendrix, wild guitarman of flames and sexual writhings, whom Joan and I saw at Monterey.

It was Jimi, a smiling bloke with a most clubbable and courteous manner whom I met two years later on a paving visit for John and Yoko in Manhattan, at some late-night hangout. I have no idea where it was, nor what it was called nor how I got there. (I was so much bolder then; I'm soberer than that, now.)

Janis Joplin was holding court. She had been at Monterey and also took off from there. Janis was always very friendly and hail-fellow. She introduced me to Jimi and said "Monterey" and "Beatles" and other passwords and I sat with her, beside Jimi and time passed and my only memory is of what can still be called "good vibes". We talked and drank, etc.

Jimi was travelling by limo then, and when the club closed (or when we closed), he dropped me off at my hotel and that was it. Not much of a story, but there you are.

He was twenty-six and utterly vulnerable, I believe. A lot of us didn't have a clue then. I was certainly old enough to know better. At this distance, I can see all the dangers. We can enjoy Jimi Hendrix and respect his memory and be glad he was around. But his life was far too short and success too dearly bought, and there are lessons for now, I hope. We must take a better care of ourselves and of each other.

Derek Taylor
East Anglia
Spring 1995

Photograph : Joseph Sia

Photograph : Mike Polillo

Prey (1967)

Despite a huge level of success and notoriety in Britain, word about the Experience had barely filtered across the Atlantic. Even after the success of their Monterey set, gigs were not easy to come by - in essence this meant the group almost starting from scratch all over again. During a run of shows at the Fillmore West, the band played a free show on the back of a flat-bed truck at the Panhandle in San Francisco's Golden Gate Park - the conquering of Jimi's homeland had begun.

"Flower power! Yeah! I wonder what we'll get next? I suppose we'll get weed-speed and then I can't wait for the winter when we'll get all those fog-songs and sledge-heads on the scene."

The Light Show (1969) Photograph : Jan Bloom / AYEI

"What followed, with respect to Carlos and Eric and all those others, was the most brilliant, emotional display of virtuoso electric guitar playing I have ever heard. I don't expect ever to hear such sustained brilliance in an hour and fifteen minutes. Jimi just stood there, did nothing - just played and played and played.'
BILL GRAHAM

From the second show that the Band Of Gypsys gave at New York's Fillmore East on New Year's Eve, 1969. This short-lived line-up - in essence the first all-black power trio - played only four complete shows. Their fifth concert, a benefit in aid of the Vietnam Moratorium Committee at Madison Square Garden, was curtailed after just two songs when Jimi, a victim of illness, had to leave the stage.

"Nowadays, too many musicians think of the money and image first before they figure out what they're trying to get across. I don't know what is happening in England but the dollar bill is God in America. All those pelican people just believe in money and nothing else. It's best not to harp upon us, the personalities and all that. It's what the whole thing is trying to get across, it's a feeling first."

We have all these different sounds, but all of them are made from just nothing but a guitar, bass and drums, and slowed-down voices.

The feedback you hear is from a straight amp and a little fuzz thing I had built. We don't even use an oscillator.

I know exactly what I'm doing when we're on stage. I don't try to move an audience - it's up to them what they get from the music.

THE VOODOO CHILE EXPERIENCE
Mick Farren

The otaku panic took hold of Zeno from the very moment that the door of his room closed behind him. He had a lot of trouble with the outside world. Had the word not hit the e-mail that the Fat Greek was selling Voodoo Chile, Zeno would never have made such a trip so early in the month. In the outside world, the sky was too vast and the people beneath it were too crowded together, too noisy and too unpredictable. The dirt, and the smell, the cumbersome randomness of external reality rasped on his anxieties. His self-preserving alarms tripped and set his heart to hammering behind a rush of desperate adrenaline. Go back inside, Zeno. You don't like it out here.

Before he could even make it through the street entrance, he had to take three or four deep and deliberate breaths to force back the flutterings. After the deep breathing, he straightened his spine under the anonymous green-drab gas cape. Walk tall, walk straight, without the otaku, shut-in cringe that all too obviously labelled you to the neanderthals as a no-problem victim. Despite all mental and physical preparation, however, he still had difficulty. From the moment that he set foot on the sidewalk and turned up his collar against prying eyes and the dreary grey drizzle that drifted down ever cyclically on the city, he had to expend a great deal of nervous energy fighting back the desire to cut and run for the safety of his fourmat, his futon and his warm dark bunker of hardware.

It wasn't that Zeno was a coward. No chicken he. In his own reality, he could be both piratical and reckless, and grin like a fool as he diced with disconnection and risked his very sanity among the fractel spikes and trick complexities on the high planes of Tracery Model or Turbo Stormcrow. Wasn't it acknowledged by the others in his pod that he was more than willing to risk suspension and even the unthinkable grounding by thumbing his nose at the Q-Sec monitors as he slipped into a closed room or bypassed a no-go? The gulf between his kind and the rest of the monkey world had simply grown too vast for effortless transition. De-evolution had washed in on the third wave and relegated the outside to television minds and dirty stunted thoughts of fear and carnage.

On the crowded Gilligan's Island of the monkey world, they communicated in grunts and fondled their diseases, and Zeno made as little contact with it or them as he possibly could. He knew, of course, that they were always out there, but, in his fourmat, in one of a million tenement conversions, the law of averages dictated that they would rarely bother him unless he actually went among them. The grocery delivered. The stipend cheques and the payments from Sony were directly deposited, and the only menu for out-venture was the replenishment of his cash and the purchase of those items, both legal and proscribed, that could not be remote-ordered on the net. In a more normal time, Zeno would not have made such a runout until maybe around the twentieth or twenty-first, but this wasn't a normal time. The Fat Greek was selling Voodoo Chile.

CHILE EXPERIENCE

For eighteen months, ever since he'd first heard tell of it, Zeno had waited for a straight shot at Voodoo Chile. No less than three times, he had believed that the elusive program was all but within his grasp. On each occasion, though, the chance had proved to be a near miss, a blind alley or a fiction. The Voodoo Chile software was all but legendary, not only on account of its rarity and the difficulty of its procurement, but also by the extent of its mondo-illegality, an illegality that superseded any Q-Sec beef of suspension and cheque stoppage. The common holding and simple possession of Voodoo Chile stood to take the entrapped or the guilty into the iron, cage-slam hideousness of Federal Agents, a three-ring judicial process that could be likened unto Kafka and a finality of hard jailtime. The reason the Feds had their nuts in a knot over Voodoo Chile and other programs of its ilk was painfully simple. Voodoo Chile had the potential of a one-way. Voodoo Chile wasn't nasty-nasty like FEC or Redrage. No sticking and hacking in Voodoo Chile. Oh no. Quite the reverse. Voodoo Chile was, by all reports and rumours, threateningly sublime. When you went into Voodoo Chile you boldly went, in all senses of the old adage, and whether you came back was anyone's guess.

As the Feds told it, Voodoo Chile, in a high sixty-two per cent of habituals, happied out the user, reducing him or her to tongue-lolling brain damage. They called it user-fatal and banned it, as they had banned Chitter and Thjong before it. They went on TV and the cheap end of the net and talked about Voodoo Chile as though it was the cybernetic equivalent of jerking off with your head in a plastic bag. The otaku knew better, of course. Those who refused to exit Voodoo Chile were only destroyed within the limited criteria of the Feds and the monkey world. Not dead but gone discorporate. The so-called brain dead explored, forever and amen, fresh and strange neuron-deep netherworlds only hinted at by the existing extreme limits.

The Fat Greek was strictly monkey world from behaviour to environment. She dealt illegal software to support a massive percodan, sucrose and polyglutamate combo habit and a pretty Eurasian boyfriend whose good looks gave him a close to religious disinclination to gainful enterprise. The first drawback was that the Fat Greek lived way over on the other side of town where the street numbers became letters and humanity ceased to be merely oppressive and turned overtly hostile with the added option of being armed. The journey to the Fat Greek's domicile was the longest piece of travelling by foot and subway that Zeno had done in many a month, and the protracted avoidance of street casual eye contact had all but drained him. The Fat Greek lived in an old-fashioned, unconverted railroad flat in a walk-up, one heater, with ragged epsilon, pass-cardies and their unmistakable stench, huddled on the landings and in the twists of the stair.

By contemporary standards the Fat Greek's apartment was spacious going on opulent, although it appeared that she rarely, if ever, emerged from the womb cocoon of her emperor-sized bed. The debris in the place was monumental and the squalor a matter of dedication. She received Zeno with no attempt at ceremony or even courtesy. Bleary on pillows, with the Eurasian asleep beside her, she was garbed in a black Victoria's Secret peignoir that revealed far more than Zeno cared to grok of her over-ample, pink-white, cellulite mountain flesh and the Glock in the shoulder holster worn next to the self-same skin.

Spaced...

Central Image : Rush & Blam
(1999)

I want to be the first man to write
about the blues scene on venus

"I want to be the first man to write about the blues scene on Venus."

The retail class, the Fat Greek and her kind, were the ones who took the brunt of the Federal heat. The sellers rather than the buyer – habituals, unless they were exceptionally careless, suffered the raids, arrests and incarcerations. In addition, the retailers frequently had no clue as to the awesome truth of their merchandise. Like this organic-indulgent, lard-pile of woman in the vast bed, they were obese immobiles, skinny tweakers or narcoleptic junkies, who favoured chemicals over connection, and were only drawn down to trade the black software by the quantum profits generated by their merch's very illegality.

The conversation was minimal. A parade of otaku whispered through her apartment at all hours of the day and night, and the Fat Greek knew the pointlessness of small talk. Zeno removed the brown bag of cash from the zippered inner pocket of his green drab and laid the soft, threadbare pile of old bills on the counterpane of her bed like a sacrificial tribute. In her turn, she took a plastic bag containing the card and a spare conversion gate from some mysterious orifice in the depths of the bed. With the transaction transacted, all that remained was the wrack of the journey home, again avoiding the eyes of the monkey world, but this time also radar tense for the echo of a Fed footfall and the authoritarian death grip. The possibility always existed that the Fat Greek was being watched.

Regaining once more the familiar security of his fourmat, Zeno was gripped by a transcendental excitement. Having shucked off his green drab, boots and bulky street clothing, he almost reverently removed the gate and the card from the plastic bag. For a full ten minutes he did nothing but squat in his underwear and stare at the two items, relishing the prospect and promise of that which was to come, and declining even to entertain the paranoia that the card might not contain Voodoo Chile at all, but merely some junk bogus program that the Fat Greek had employed to rob him. That he could be ripped in this way was all but unthinkable. He doubted that his karma could be in such negative balance and the Fat Greek, although unsavoury in person, had a reputation to maintain that she would hardly jeopardise by working a cheap switch. Unless, of course, the jones had pushed to some short-term wickedness of deception. With addicts, that eventuality could always cloud a transaction.

Zeno was aware that, to some extent, he was avoiding the moment of truth. The proof was in the perception and he had to proceed to perceive. His movements were almost casual as he snapped the Voodoo Chile card into the external port of the old and heavily customised NK Alpha that served him as a master controller. He waited while it loaded. Outwardly he showed no more emotion than if he'd been routinely laundry listing. His movements were swift, precise, revealing nothing of his conflicted inner turmoil. Finally, the primary screen cleared and the equivalent of a copyright box appeared.

THIS PROGRAM IS A FULL SENSORY
CREATION OF THE BLACK AVENGER.
BEHOLD YOU MORTALS AND TREMBLE.

Zeno understood that Black Avenger boasted not idly. Legend-word was that it had been he, back in his wild days, who had shit canned the entire air traffic control at Templehof, and taken the karma for the resultant airwreck passenger massacre. This notice remained for some ten seconds and then was replaced by a second.

THIS PROGRAM IS BASED ON THE MUSICAL WORK VOODOO CHILE BY JIMI HENDRIX RENDERED TO A TOTAL SENSORY EXPERIENCE BY THE BLACK AVENGER. (BEHOLD YOU MORTALS etc.)

The second was replaced by a third. This time, it was a quasi-copyright warning. Most black programs were preceded by a disclaimer of this kind.

USE OF THIS PROGRAM HAS BEEN DEEMED ILLEGAL UNDER THE FULL SANCTION OF FEDERAL AND LOCAL LAW. AS SUCH, IT IS NOT PROTECTED BY CONVENTIONAL COPYRIGHT PROTOCOLS, BUT UNAUTHORISED COPYING AND MISUSE CAN RESULT IN SUDDEN AND VIOLENT RETRIBUTION.

The warning then gave way to just three words.

POWER MADE ABSOLUTE.

The three words flashed three times and then faded. A new window appeared.

CONNECT RECEIVERS NOW.

The instruction was redundant. The Packard Bell exosuit that was Zeno's main receiver always remained connected. When he wasn't actually experiencing it, it sat hunched on its stand like a dark blue, inert crustacean, silent, but on line and ready. Dressing in the suit was one of Zeno's few true tactile contacts that he wholly relished. He drew on the torso unit, the legs and sleeves, the gloves and finally bowed his head to the crowning disorientation of the first few moments in the helmet as the real retreated and the virtual became his all. Initially, he had the tunnel effect, but then his senses settled and the falling sensation left him along with the easy concepts of up, down and depth. He drifted in a ready room, in a magnet breeze of proto-colour and shoals of random, spiralling pixels.

FLEX RIGHT GLOVE TO PROCEED.
(Yes) No.

Zeno's right hand snapped to a fist, and all was made black in the first impenetrable absence. The final tease of anticipation and the ever-present start-up uncertainty that nothing would happen and he would remain to eternity, starvation or death, windwalking in nothingness. And then tiny flecks of light rushing at him from a great silent distance. The light came as heralds to the sound, drawing up from the silence, the first rustling wah wah chicken pecks rising in volume and then the solo Jimi primal theme, closing around his inertia and guiding him forward through the entry system, drifting him surely through apertures in great floating ideograms of polished steel, that exhorted him to pay attention, as they rose over the infinite curved parallels of the virtual horizon like huge irregular and vertical airships, unreadable but known and certain, obvious in their courses and meanings. (Damn, but the Black Avenger was. Good. Brilliant. Awesome.) The theme repeated, liquid blue splashes of high-hat and the blossoming of tentative percussion. A cartoon sign hammered into its own cratered space rock, much in the manner of when Bugs Bunny had his encounters with the invading Martians, bore the words

WAIT FOR IT, SCHMUCK!

The full-bore power hit like breaking tsunami. Even expected, it came as a shock of joy and Zeno was spin curled and hurled – although precious little of his Zeno identity was happening at that point – to drown or ride the wave. For an instant he caught a culture back blossom, a flash from the time of Hendrix. Zeno was the chromium man hanging chromium ten on the chromium board, and the vision stabilised his forward motion. But Silver Surfing was too crude for anything but instantaneous adjustment in a Black Avenger creation. Literacy split and he was an electron entity, slipsliding and pinballing the magnetic field of a Stratocaster as big as a galaxy, micro through macro, and Marshall stacks like the monoliths of distant watching guardians. The bass line pulsed beneath him, a dark double helix boring in to the rock of ages. (While somewhere in a marginal note, Wesley Snipes argued with Woody Harrelson, in the movie White Men Can't Jump, *that Jimi's rhythm section was never ever white, never in a million years, you dumb ass, hillbilly motherfucker.)*

The magnetic fields turned schematic, a switchback grid of undulating blue lines and crackling force plasma that he railrode by the dictates of a baroque and capriciously shifting gravity. Robert Johnson, Johnny Shines, Little Richard's Daddy and Maitre Ka-Fu (the Master of the Crossroads) waited at the initial intersection, at Blue Bayou, offering a jug of white lightning and the option to branch to roots, but Zeno highballed on by. Maybe as a part of some later excursion. In the neophyte time, stay the main course.

WELL I'M STANDING
NEXT TO A MOUNTAIN
CHOP IT DOWN WITH
THE EDGE OF MY HAND

Tectonic plates shifted uncomfortably and Alps split their faultlines as Atlas shrugged. The tiny women sang and Mothra woke on Monster Island. Boulders big as asteroids cascaded down to geo-apocalypse, now and forever, and formative planets gathered debris greedy for the first critical mass. (Damn, but the Black Avenger was. Something.) Boulders rose and fragments re-formed, knitting together into cellular coherency. Zeno no longer surfed. He was momentarily adrift upon a summer sea. Lazy lotus islands idled past on siren sighs beneath a purple velvet void. The great flux became a single curving swell and Zeno's entirety was suffused with a golden sun-warmth and all anxiety fell away, but then the light began to fade in a tropical sunset, coloured like love's adoring bruise, and an edge of excitement energised him to a new expectancy. Bright letters of fire, jagged as the mark of Zorro, streaked across the now indigo sky, whipping him on like the reason why.

BECAUSE I'M A VOODOO CHILE, I'M A VOODOO CHILE.

Pathways formed to the edge of night, and Zeno knew that he had entered a new phase and a new depth. A curving, colonnaded avenue, that was perhaps some mighty fragment

PHOTOGRAPHY : Joseph Sia

Courtesy : AYEI

Sometimes you see things in different ways than other people,
so then you write it in a song. It could represent anything.
Like some feelings make you think of different colours. Jealousy is purple,
I'm purple with rage or purple with anger - and green is envy.

We shouldn't have to keep carrying the old burdens around. You have to be a freak in order to be different. And them freaks are very prejudiced. You have to talk in a certain way in order to be with them, and in order to be with the others, you have to wear your hair short and wear a tie. So we're trying to make a third world happen...

I'm working on my next album for late summer release. It will be called Shine On Earth, Shine On or Gypsy Sun. There's a great need for harmony between man and earth. I think we are really screwing up that harmony by dumping garbage in the sea and air pollution and all that stuff. And the sun is very important. It's what keeps everything alive.

The truth shall be known to all. The will to accept the truth must be fed, never suspiciously bled. People must never be afraid of paths chosen by God. In their hearts they see the path so much more clearly and truthfully than through the eyes. Love is being tested here, not just of our families, for our WHOLE world. The time has come for us to be on the watch, to know the scent, to recognise, to stand and visualise, stand and realise.

Race isn't a problem in my world. I don't look at things in terms of races. I look at things in terms of people. I just want to do what I'm doing without getting involved in racial or political matters. I know I'm lucky that I can do that - lots of people can't.

I sacrifice part of my soul every time I play. The moment I feel that I don't have anything more to give musically, that's when I won't be found on this planet, unless I have a wife and children, because if I don't have anything to communicate through my music, then there is nothing for me to live for. I'm not sure I will live to be twenty-eight years old.

The background of our music is a spiritual blues thing. Now I want to bring it down to earth. I want to get back to the blues, because that's what I am.

Photograph : Linda McCartney

S'cuse me, while I kiss the sky

Am I happy or in misery?
Whatever it is that girl put a
spell on me

Help me! Help me!

Is it tomorrow, or just the end
of time?

(Purple Haze)

Outward Bound (1992)
Art : Ian Wright

By 1969 Jimi Hendrix doesn't want to know about burning his guitar, or putting on onstage displays of gymnastics:

Listen to the motherfucker or leave the hall. And so people do start to listen. Critically, however, there is a downside: the phenomenon of Jimi Hendrix is out of favour; he is considered possibly burnt out.

The internal frictions are proving too much. Noel Redding quits and returns to England. Mitch Mitchell also leaves the band but soon returns to take his place among the pool of musicians Hendrix is assembling. Jimi, meanwhile, has contacted his old friend Billy Cox and persuades him to leave Nashville. Cox's solid, more funky bass style is to be a crucial part of Hendrix's new music.

> *I'm not sure how I feel about the Experience now. I died a thousand times in that group and was born again. But after a while you have to get yourself straightened out. Maybe we could have gone on but what would have been the point of that, what would it have been good for? It's a ghost now – it's dead, like back pages in a diary. I'm into new things and I want to think about tomorrow, not yesterday.*

In a little less than eighteen months the Jimi Hendrix Experience have released three of the most epochal albums in contemporary music. In this burst of creative energy are expressed many of the songs that have lain dormant in Jimi's creative psyche ever since he started to express the musical ideas boiling and bubbling within him.

A new level now has been reached, however: the public has woken up to him – now he can start dreaming. And there are many more works within him that require a more studied approach than what up until now essentially has been a primal outpouring of art. Financially secure beyond his wildest dreams, Jimi now turns his attention to these larger concepts. He has had ideas for working with orchestras, employing great soundscapes and soundwashes to summon up the music within his head. Unable to read and write musical scores, however, he will scribble out an arrangement in long hand: "at this point the guitar plays three notes … " If he doesn't write out new compositions in this way, the only means to prevent them vanishing into the ether is to rush into the studio and immediately record them. All the same, Jimi begins to feel frustrated about his lack of orthodox musical training, and plans in the near future to learn to write music formally. He needs to start expanding and satisfying all the ideas that he has.

Music that goes even beyond jazz is now at the forefront of Jimi's attention. "I hear sounds in my head and if I don't get them together, then no one will," he says. Around the same time Jimi is introduced to the producer Alan Douglas, who soon becomes a close friend. Through the course of the year they work on various projects including the soon-to-be-unveiled musical collective, the Band Of Gypsys.

> *It's more than music. It is like church, like a foundation for the potentially lost. We're making music into a new kind of Bible, a Bible you can carry in your hearts. One that will give you a physical feeling. You hypnotise people to where they go back to their natural state which is pure positive, like in childhood when you get natural highs. Everything is electrified nowadays. That is why the name Electric Church flashes in and out. When I get up on stage and sing, that's my whole life. THAT is my religion. I am Electric Religion.*

Thus resolved within himself, the songwriting of Jimi Hendrix becomes even more extraordinary. Many of his songs until now have had a linear structure: although highly achieved and beautiful as they are in their own right, Jimi will refer to tunes like "Purple Haze" or "Crosstown Traffic" as his "cartoon songs". Works like "Cherokee Mist", however, are constructed almost on classical lines, built around progressions and movements. Even earlier songs like "Castles Made Of Sand", with its musical evolution and reprises, suggest such complexities as are to come. "1983, a Merman I Should Turn To Be", meanwhile, is a similar signpost that here we are dealing with a master composer; apart from its extraordinary subject-matter – not many songs had previously had lyrics about living underwater – it is a musically inspired composition, with Jimi exploring musical places you would not think would be available within the structure of the song.

In fact, the lyrical subject-matter of "1983" is in many ways as unique as the song's musical context. Science fiction premises and the imagination of science-fiction writers truly inspire Jimi: the presupposition of non-real existence is where he is coming from, one foot in this world and one in the next for as long as he is on this planet this time around.

And in songs like "Third Stone From The Sun" there is real wit in his words: Jimi returns to earth and the most intelligent thing he finds there are chickens. Where does this shit come from? Not, certainly, from the acid he would regularly ingest – Jimi wouldn't be taken places by acid; he'd tell the acid where to take him. No, Jimi's poetic thinking is harnessed to a mind naturally attuned to science fiction. He is bored beyond belief by the mundane aspects of life. Which is why all the time he runs to his beloved guitars. And he is still only in his mid-twenties.

The rush of ideas is constant. It never stops, never lets up. In mid-conversation his eyes will all of a sudden rise upwards as he spaces out on the latest creative flash that has shot through him. The ideas are impossible to control, and never give him a break. All the time, he is thinking about his music – new songs, new ideas. Sometimes this inability to stop the flow of creativity becomes nerve-racking, draining.

Alan Douglas's jazz connections provide fresh avenues of musical explorations. It is through Douglas that one of the most intriguing projects is proposed: a Jimi Hendrix/Miles Davis album. Alas, the idea founders because of Miles's financial demands.

In August 1969 Jimi Hendrix appears at the Woodstock Music And Art Fair in upstate New York, playing with the Band Of Gypsys, a loose pool of musicians. "We decided to change the whole thing around and call it Gypsy Sun And Rainbows," Jimi announces on stage. "For short it is nothing but a Band Of Gypsys." Hendrix's Band Of Gypsys features Mitch Mitchell, Billy Cox, rhythm guitarist Larry Lee with Juma Sultan and Jerry Velez on percussion.

Woodstock is the biggest celebration of the counter-culture, billed as *three days of peace and music*. The organisers have reckoned on an audience of 100,000 people; in the event nearly 500,000 attend. The massive logistical problems, compounded by dramatic and torrential rainfall, mean the festival overruns disastrously.

It is intended that Jimi will go on stage at eleven o'clock at night and close the festival. In the manner of all things at Woodstock, however, he is interminably delayed … Although, in the end, it seems that in this endless procrastination about when Jimi will appear on stage there is some form of divine plan. By the time he steps out onto the boards at 7.30 in the morning, the spectacle is magnificent: the sun is rising; contrasted against it, the festival site looks and smells like a war zone.

Unveiling his new line-up for the first time, the show is initially ragged – Jimi had not been well as he waited for his slot in the show finally to arrive. But then he hits "The Starspangled Banner". The Band Of Gypsys' impressionistic performance of the American national song is like the manifesto of the new time they are ushering in, ripping up the anthem's traditional values and reshaping them with utopian passion. It seems as though a coup has taken place in humanity's collective soul. This wordless performance, delivered at the height of America's civil rights unrest and Vietnam War turmoil, is a compelling and eloquent statement. The new music that follows on for the rest of the set reveals itself as magical, floating, clearly inspired from on high. Jimi becomes a pure poet of his instrument. "I have plans that are unbelievable," he has promised.

> *With the Experience there was more room for ego-tripping. All I had to blast off the stage was the drummer and the bass player. Now I want to step back and let other things come forward.*

> *Woodstock was groovy. The non-violence, the very true brand of music. The acceptance of the crowd, how they had to sleep in the mud and the rain and get hassled by this and that. There's so many scores you can add up on this thing. If you added them all up you'd feel like a king. I'd like for everybody to see this kind of festival, see how everybody mixed together in harmony.*

Jimi hangs in New York. He takes an apartment downtown, on Sixth and Twelfth. At the Record Plant he takes a block booking, although he rarely arrives to work there much before midnight. In the evenings he'll turn up at Alan Douglas's house and listen to his stories about Charlie Mingus and Art Blakey and Coltrane and Miles; Douglas is producing the Last Poets, perhaps the first rap record, and Jimi is fascinated by this, even recording with Jalal, the group's leader.

On New Year's Eve, the Band Of Gypsys play the Fillmore East in New York. The group is now a trio, with Buddy Miles and Billy Cox featuring in an all-black line-up. The shows (the group also play on New Year's Day) are recorded and result in the Band Of Gypsys' album, released in April. It includes an exceptional performance of Hendrix's strident anti-war song "Machine Gun".

> *That first set was really tight. It was scary. Buddy's going to do most of the singing from now on. I'd rather just play.*

On January 28 the Band Of Gypsys headline a benefit concert for the Vietnam Moratorium Committee at New York's Madison Square Garden. Hendrix, however, has to leave the stage after two numbers, a victim of illness. The show is, coincidentally, the last performance by this line-up.

Through the summer months of 1970 Hendrix plays the Cry Of Love tour in America. His rhythm section has now stabilised as Mitch Mitchell and Billy Cox and among the dates are appearances at Berkeley, Rainbow Bridge in Hawaii and the Atlanta Pop Festival. This line-up of the Band Of Gypsys is burning, Mitchell and Cox proving to be Jimi's finest rhythm section. Never intimidated by Jimi, as other drummers often are, Mitch drives the group, as Billy Cox feeds Jimi bass-lines. And the guitar that Jimi is playing is extraordinary.

> *When I was in Hawaii I saw a beautiful thing … a miracle. There were lots of rings around the moon and the rings were all women's faces. I wish I could tell someone about it.*

Hendrix is also working overtime in the recording studio. He is planning another double album, to be called *First Rays Of The New Rising Sun*, that is to be a reflection of the profound musical level he is working at – part of it is released as *The Cry Of Love*. He is also starting to write music for a big band, "a new form of classical music".

The idea for Jimi to have his own

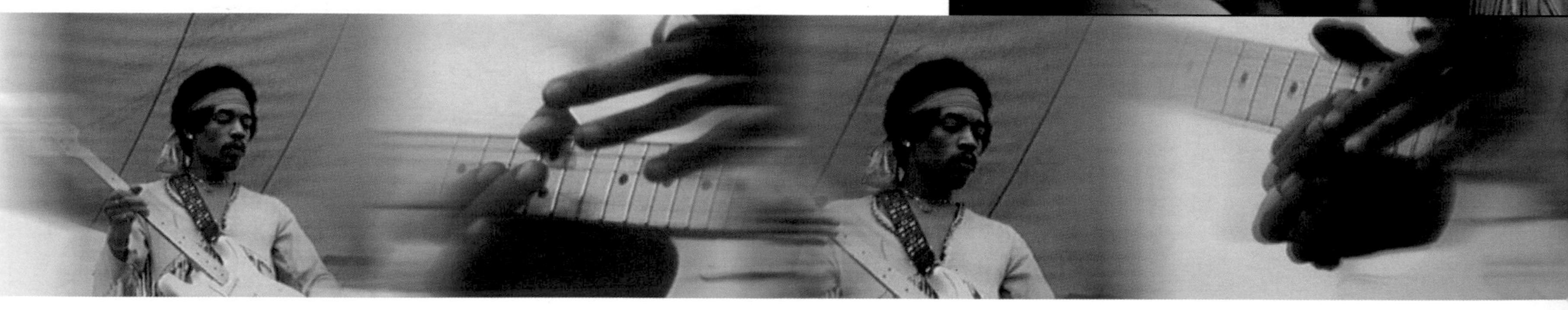

Woodstock: the most talked-about festival in the history of rock and the biggest celebration ever of the counter-culture was billed as three days of peace and music. The initial plan had been to hold the festival in Walkill, New York but, a month before the event, the show was banned. David Byrd, famed for his Fillmore East work, had already created a poster but the forced relocation called for a new one - fast. Arnold Skolnik's poster was produced in several permutations since many of the headline acts only confirmed as the weekend drew nearer, thus this is the Final Edition Woodstock Poster. Held at Max Yasgur's farm in Bethel, the festival attracted just short of half a million people - the organisers had reckoned on a maximum crowd capacity of 100,000. Massive logistical problems, compounded by torrential rainstorms, meant that it dramatically over ran: Jimi was originally invited to headline the final night but he finally made it on stage at 7.30 a.m. the following morning, debuting his new band. Delivered at the height of America's civil rights unrest and Vietnam War turmoil, his wordless deconstruction of "The Star-Spangled Banner", was as compelling, eloquent and relevant a statement then as it is now, more than a generation later.

"The so-called other generation have a way of over-protecting their young. Younger people, their minds are keener and since they can't get release and respect from older people, their music gets louder and rebellious. They look up to us quicker than they'll look up to what the President says. They're tired of joining street gangs, they're tired of joining militant groups, they're tired of hearing the President gab his gums away. That's why you had a lot of people at Woodstock."

Clip: Star Spangled. M [1]

Woodstock - Side Stage (1969)
Photograph : Allan Koss

"I see that we meet again! We got tired of Experience so we decided to change the whole thing around and call it Gypsys Sun and Rainbows. For short, it's nothing but a Band Of Gypsys. We have Billy Cox playing bass from Nashville, Tennessee. Larry Lee playing guitar over there and Juma playing congas over here. We have a heart, Mitch Mitchell on drums and we got Jerry Velez on congas too. Yours truly on meat whistle! Alright... give us a minute to tune up.... before we go any further I'd like to say you proved to the world what could happen with a little bit of love and understanding. Now... gimme an A, I'll pay you back!"

I covered Woodstock both front and back stage. The only time I actually go ON stage was as Jimi came on. I guess, by then, that the pass system had broken down because no one cared too much that I was there. The lasting impression I have is of how in awe I was of his performance. Maybe because of that I actually shot very few pictures!
ALAN KOSS

Stealing a pick-up truck with Jimi at Woodstock is one of the high points of my life. He was at one with his instrument, no one else had brought the electric guitar to that level; no one has since. It was like handstands above everyone else, so liquid. Absolutely the best guitar player that ever lived; there's no one even in the same building as that guy. You gotta preserve Jimi and don't let him rust away any more now. NEIL YOUNG

studio has been percolating since 1968, in essence because of his habit of block-booking the Record Plant at peak rates. Jamming in the studio is not a cost-effective exercise at the best of times and Jimi's recording expenses mount at a simply astronomical rate. Plans for the new studio, Electric Lady, are drawn up in conjunction with Jimi's long-time recording associate Eddie Kramer. The state-of-the-art facility – red carpeting, curved white walls, a floating ceiling with a remote-controlled theatrical lighting system plus film projection suite – opens for business in August 1970.

There is one thing I hate about studios and that is the impersonality of them. They are cold and blank and within a few minutes I lose all drive and inspiration. Electric Lady is different. It has been built with great atmosphere so it makes people feel like they are recording at home. I want it to be an oasis for all the rock musicians in New York.

I'm working on my own album which will have about twenty tracks on it. It will be a double set again and some tracks are getting very long. But, you see, our music doesn't pertain to one thing. You don't have to be singing about love all the time in order to give love.

At the same time Jimi and Alan Douglas are working on a jazz collaboration with the great arranger Gil Evans, whose work with Miles Davis provides some of the landmark albums of contemporary music. They agree to embark on the project once Hendrix has returned from his European tour that autumn. It is to be called *Voodoo Child Plays The Blues*, and it is intended that Jimi will stand up in front of an orchestra and play, as Miles had done with Evans on *Sketches Of Spain* and *Miles Ahead*.

Jimi and the Cry Of Love band arrive in England at the end of August. Their only UK date is a headlining appearance at the Isle of Wight Festival, an event soured by tensions and bad weather.

It is followed by a week of European concerts during which Cox is handed a drink spiked with LSD. He has a traumatically bad reaction and the group's final dates are scrapped. Hendrix brings Cox back to London where he can recover away from the pressures of touring.

I'm thinking of the days when people will be able to have this little room, a total audio-visual environment type of thing. So that you can go in there and lay back and the whole thing just blossoms with colour and sound. Like a reflection room. You can just go in and jingle out your nerves. It would be incredible if you could produce music so perfect that it would filter through you like rays and ultimately cure.

Hendrix stays in London with a girlfriend, Monika Danneman. He does the social rounds, and jams with Eric Burdon and War at Ronnie Scott's Club.

I am planning a world tour and this will be either before or after Christmas. There are lots of places we want to play. I want to go to Japan and Australia. We really want to come back to England and do one big concert at each of the major cities.

On the night of September 17, Jimi takes some sleeping pills, so he can sleep through the next day and leave London the following Monday.

I want to wake up in the morning and just roll out of my bed into an indoor pool, swim to the breakfast table, come up for air and maybe get a drink of orange juice and … you know … a shave. Is that luxurious? I was thinking about a tent, maybe overhanging a mountain stream.

Early the next morning Danneman notices Jimi has vomited during the night. He seems to be breathing normally, however, and she feels no reason to panic. A little later she tries to wake him but Jimi remains unconscious. This time Danneman is really alarmed. She calls an ambulance.

On September 18, 1970, after a European tour, Jimi's soul reunites with the cosmos. His last and greatest trip.

> *My goal is to be one with the music. I just dedicate my whole life to this art ... Something new has got to come, and Jimi Hendrix will be there.*

> *I attribute my success to God. It all comes from God. I go by message. I'm really a messenger from God. My name is nothing but a distraction. Forget my name. Remember it only as a handshake.*

(1970)

1 8 . 0 9 .

Artists, Photographers and Writers

JOHN ADLER

Photographed Jimi backstage at the Los Angeles Forum at the end of April 1970 - the opening night of the Cry Of Love tour.

JAN BLOOM

Jan Bloom moved from his native Holland to America in the late 1960s and became house photographer at Bill Graham's Fillmore East in New York. Bloom remained on the East Coast, working as a freelance until the early 1980s before moving back to Holland where he now contributes to major Dutch publications.

LAURA BOOMER

Laura Boomer shared Jimi Hendrix's fascination with the cosmos. Her interest in astrology, however, began while pursuing an art school education. After working with art department styling costumes for film, TV and video, Laura turned her hobby into a career. In 1990 she co-created and hosted Channel Four's notable *Astrology Show*. Since then she has written for numerous magazines, newspapers and periodicals and appeared on many TV and radio shows. She performs as Aura Beau, gives workshops, maintains a private practice, and is currently editing her astrological handbook entitled *Found in Space.*

ADRIAN BOOT

Curator and Art Director of the Jimi Hendrix Exhibition and the Bob Marley Songs Of Freedom Exhibition, Adrian Boot graduated from Surrey University before moving to Jamaica to teach physics in the early 1970s, returning to Britain to freelance for the *NME, Melody Maker, The Times* and *Guardian.* By the mid-1970s he had become staff photographer for *Melody Maker*. Moving on, he has been: chief photographer for Live Aid; for Nelson Mandela: Freedom at 70; for Roger Waters' The Wall in Berlin; for Greenpeace in the former Soviet Union. He has also worked with ORBIS, the flying eye hospital, in Africa; the British Council in Iraq and Jordan; and for the Grateful Dead in Egypt; as well as for Island Records in Jamaica, Colombia and many other parts of the world.

His books include *Jah Revenge* and Babylon *On A Thin Wire* (both with Michael Thomas), *Live Aid* and *The Secret Policeman's Ball*, as well as *Bob Marley: Natural Mystic* (with Vivien Goldman), *Midnights in Moscow,* a study of the Soviet Union (with Chris Salewicz), *International Reggae* (with Peter Simon) and (with Chris Salewicz) *Bob Marley: Songs Of Freedom* (published by Bloomsbury/Viking). Since building his own computer in 1976, Boot has been increasingly at the blunt end of computer technology. The founder of Exhibit-A, Adrian Boot works in a variety of formats and mental states.

RICHARD BULL

Richard Bull was born in London in 1968 and studied Graphic Design at the Chelsea School of Art for some 5 years during the late eighties, early nineties. A product of the digital revolution, his first interactions with processing units began at an early age, producing 'Hi-Res' linear drawing on basic late 70's Research Machines. Joining Stylorouge in 1992 he immediately began to work on Alan Douglas' famed Jimi Hendrix projects, including *The Ultimate Experience* and *Blues* Albums, the *On The Road Again Tour* and now as Senior Designer for this publication. He is married to a Southern Californian, a 'digital darling' in her own right and they share their home with an ever growing 4ft long Green Iguana.

ED CARAEFF

Ed Caraeff is a West Coast photographer whose best-known image is that of Jimi setting his guitar on fire at Monterey. Caraeff hung out with the West Coast crowd, hence his on-the-spot ability to capture Jimi playing pool at John and Michelle Phillips' house, where Jimi stayed shortly after the Monterey show. Caraeff's Fire Works picture was also used in 1987 as a cover illustration for *Rolling Stone* magazine.

JEAN NOEL COGHE

A French journalist who worked for *Rock et Folk*, the country's premier music magazine, Coghe was the first mainstream French rock writer to interview Jimi Hendrix. Coghe was also an amateur photographer who would shoot his own pictures on assignment. He is currently European Radio Correspondent for the RTL radio network, covering northern France.

IRA COHEN

Photographer, poet, film-maker, historian and publisher, Ira Cohen was born in New York during 1935 to deaf-mute parents. In 1961 he took a Yugoslavian freighter to Tangier where he lived for four years and published *Gnaoua*, a magazine devoted to exorcism. In the late sixties, Cohen created Mylar Images, an awesome body of surrealistic photographs. During this time he also directed the movie, *Thunderbolt Pagoda* and produced *Paradise Now*, a film of Julian Beck's 1968 Living Theatre tour. He has travelled extensively in Ethiopia and India where he photographed the Kumbh Mela. Cohen's books of poetry include *Poems From The Cosmic Crypt* and *The Stauffenberg Cycle.* He has exhibited his photographs in Japan, New York and, most recently, in London.

Photograph : Joseph Sia

CAROLINE COON

Caroline Coon was born in London in 1945, and educated at the Legat Russian Ballet School. She dropped out of Central School of Art in 1967 to found the twenty-four hour release and legal advice service, Release. In 1971 she was one of the women to whom Germaine Greer dedicated *The Female Eunuch* - and since 1972 she has lived in France, Morocco, North America and the Caribbean, writing and painting. The always revolutionary and progressive force of popular culture that revives and enlivens art is at the heart of her work.

DAVID COSTA

Born in 1947, Costa paid lip-service to a study of fine arts at the University of East Anglia before lying his way into the music industry. An association with DJM in 1972 led to a sequence of album sleeves for Elton John: he collaborated on the design of the *Goodbye Yellow Brick Road* album before art directing and designing sleeves for *Single Man, Blue Moves, Jump Up, Reg Strikes Back, Sleeping With The Past, The Very Best Of EJ* and *To Be Continued*, which won the 1992 Music Week Special Packaging Award. Costa has also prepared album sleeves for George Harrison (*Cloud Nine*, with Gered Mankowitz), the Travelling Wilburys and Eric Clapton (in conjunction with Peter Blake). His design work for *Blinds & Shutters*, Michael Cooper's collection, gained him many plaudits. David Costa runs Wherefore Art, a design group in London.

MICK FARREN

Mick Farren first saw Jimi Hendrix, playing "Hey Joe", on *Ready Steady Go!* in the winter of 1966 and instantly realised a positive quantum step was being achieved in popular music. Around that time, Farren was first putting together the notorious Social Deviants who dedicated themselves to never taking a positive step in any direction. Since that time, he has made a half-dozen albums, written some fifteen novels, published seven works of non-fiction (including no less than four books on Elvis Presley) and a slim volume of poetry. He has created two award-winning documentaries and even written songs for Motorhead. Formerly, he was editor of *International Times*, and a contributing editor of *New Musical Express* in its mid-seventies' heyday.

MARK FRENCH and BILL WOOD

Mark is presently a director for video and theatre as well as being studio manager at Red Bus Studios. Bill Wood is owner of Taste TV Productions; an independent music video label specialising in techno and psychedelic music. Wood is a producer, editor, cameraman, computer animator and graphic artist.

CAESAR GLEBBEEK

Dutch-born Caesar Glebbeek founded the Jimi Hendrix Information Centre in 1967. It contains over 10,000 articles and reviews, tapes of interviews, concerts and studio sessions, and databanks of information detailing all aspects of Jimi's life. With Harry Shapiro, he is co-author of *Electric Gypsy*, the definitive book on the life of Jimi Hendrix. Caesar edits *Univibes*, The International Jimi Hendrix Magazine, and lives in Cork, Ireland.

RICK GRIFFIN

Rick Griffin is recognised as one of the most influential West Coast poster artists of all time. Acknowledged for his comic art - most notably the character Murph The Surf - and founder of the ZAP Comix series, Rick's work is characterised by a richness of imagery that always contains multiple meanings. Griffin drew from many sources and utilised superlative draughtmanship, word play, sexual and insect-like imagery, all underpinned by an indefinable mysticism. By fusing his creativity with actual event information, Griffin created an electrifying body of work with landmark designs for the Grateful Dead, the Doors, and Jefferson Airplane among many others; more recently, he worked with REM and Siouxsie and the Banshees. His acknowledged masterpiece, *The Eyeball*, dates from 1968. Rick died tragically from injuries sustained following a motorcycle accident near his home in California on August 17, 1991.

DOUGLAS KENT HALL

Educated at the University of Utah, Douglas Kent Hall has had a wide and varied career that has encompassed advertising and rock 'n' roll while also working as a contributor for the likes of *Playboy, Vogue, Le Matin, Art Forum* and *Vanity Fair*. Hall moved to London in 1968 before relocating to New York the following year when his book *Rock: A World Bold As Love* was published. Further photo-essays and novels were published through the seventies and eighties. His film work includes *The Great American Cowboy*, which won an Academy Award in 1974. Hall has exhibited in many of the most prestigious galleries in North America. In 1989 he worked in Brazil on a book and film portraying miners in the rain forest. The next year he travelled to Britain to begin chronicling people who live on Dartmoor. In 1991, he travelled to St Petersburg and Moscow in collaboration with the Hermitage Museum to photograph the New Russia. Douglas Kent Hall lives in New Mexico.

DEZO HOFFMAN

Dezo Hoffman was born in Czechoslovakia and graduated in photo-journalism from Prague University. On becoming a newsreel photographer for 20th Century Fox in Paris, Hoffman covered the Spanish Civil War, working alongside Ernest Hemingway. Enlisting in the Czech army, he covered the World War Two as a news cameraman. His war work has since been donated to the Imperial War Museum. Hoffman is more famous for his celebrity pictures: Charlie Chaplin, Marilyn Monroe, Frank Sinatra, Louis Armstrong, Marlene Dietrich, the Beatles, Jimi Hendrix, Phil Spector, the Rolling Stones and many, many more. In 1955 he joined *Record Mirror*, where he remained for twenty years while still freelancing for most of Fleet Street. A trip to Liverpool in 1963 saw the start of a relationship with the Beatles, whereby he became their unofficial chief photographer for the first eighteen months of their career. Dezo Hoffman died in 1986; in just over thirty years he had assembled a priceless and timeless archive of over one million negatives which have since become the source of a multitude of pictorial biographies.

GRAHAM HOWE

A London based photographer who worked in the late 1960s, primarily for the *NME* and *Melody Maker* and alongside Joe Andrews (now Joe of Joe's Basement), was one of a handful of photographers prepared to shoot from the hip, photographing those who were on the cutting edge and many more who aspired to be. His most notable sessions were with Pink Floyd and Cream. Graham Howe has since left photography and is a four-colour print planner living in London.

iQ VIDEOGRAPHICS

The London-based company was formed in 1985 and the following year installed the world's first Quantel Paintbox. iQ's clients include British Telecom, the Royal Mail, British Rail, Simple Minds and Bob Marley.

w/bar
Fdbk.t.s.(N)t.s.(B)
t.s.(B) Fdbk.
Fdbk. pitches:E,F♯
Fdbk. pitch:D
(D is most prominant pitch)
it rain___ fall
grad. release grad. release
Yeah!
full
P.M.
Feedback
Would I be truth - ful, yeah,__
(end Rhy. Fig. 1)
Let me
D(add9)
fire!
Let me stand
Whoa,__ let me

PROFESSOR GUNTHER KIESER

Gunther Kieser was born in 1930 in Kronberg, Germany. He was fifteen when the Allies liberated the country from Nazi tyranny: "From then on I was able to hear the strange music from the USA." From 1949 to the present day Kieser has designed all the jazz and rock concert and festival posters for promoters Lippmann & Rau. He created the Medusa Head poster for Jimi Hendrix's 1969 tour of Germany."The expression of this portrait with the strong hair around his face was like a human signal. I was sure the audience would understand this as a visual translation of Jimi and his music." Kieser's art has been exhibited all over the world. Since 1980, he has been Professor of Communications and Design at the Bergische University, Wuppertal.

MATI KLARWEIN

Mati Klarwein's life started with a blinding flash of sunlight and hot sand on his lips. His mother was a conceptual artist who conceived him as a public art event on the afternoon beaches of Jerusalem - on the very spot where East and West fuck and fight - surrounded by a larger circle of flames and an even larger circle of undulating grimaces of the bearded Bedouins in the heatwaves. He stepped out of his mother's womb with a spray-can of paint in his hand and running to the Wailing Wall, he proceeded to cover it with graffiti of all the possible combinations of all the letters in all of the different alphabets in the world. At this very moment he is sitting in his studio writing his own.

ALLAN KOSS

A freelance photojournalist, Allan Koss covered Woodstock for the underground newspaper, the *Chicago Seed*. Today, Koss still lives and works in Chicago as a contributor to various publications while specialising in the social issues of the mid-west. "I feel very privileged now to have participated in four days of the Woodstock Music Festival. You could feel 'historic' in the making. For the final act - Jimi 'Purple Haze' Hendrix - I had finally made it on the stage using my *Chicago Seed* press pass and stood where millions of others would have liked to have been."

ELLIOTT LANDY

Born in 1942, Elliott started photography in Europe but returned to his native America in 1967. Through the years he has shot LP covers for Bob Dylan (*Nashville Skyline*), the Band (*The Band*), Van Morrison (*Moondance*), Big Brother (*Cheap Thrills*) and Ornette Coleman (*Ornette at 12*). He has also covered most of the major music events over the past 25 years, and his published books include *Woodstock Vision*. Elliott Landy has exhibited in galleries around the world, while his work has been acquired by La Bibliothéque Nationale in Paris, the Canadian Film board and private collectors. Elliott Landy is currently developing a project of interactive music video, shooting material on film and processing it as videotape.

JEAN-PIERRE LELOIR

The photographic career of Jean-Pierre Leloir began in 1945, when, at the age of fourteen, he was given a baby Brownie camera by a GI in newly liberated Paris. Five years later he replaced it with his first Rolleiflex, and began to take photographs of visiting American jazz musicians in the French capital. Over the next decades he was present at many of the most significant left-field arts events in France and the world, as well as taking advertising pictures for such giants as Shell. In 1966, the year he became involved in the setting up of the seminal French publication, *Rock Et Folk*, he met Jimi Hendrix on his first trip to France. In 1982 he shot his twenty thousandth reel of film at the Nice Festival of Jazz.

LINDA McCARTNEY

Inspired by the work of Walker Evans and Dorothea Laing, the young Linda Eastman's big break came in 1966 when she photographed the Rolling Stones on a yacht on New York's Hudson River. She went on to assemble a portfolio that reads like a who's who of seminal rock artists: the Beatles, the Who, the Doors, Neil Young, Otis Redding, BB King, Grateful Dead, the Byrds, Frank Zappa and Jimi Hendrix. Linda McCartney was house photographer at Bill Graham's Fillmore East and also became *Rolling Stone* magazine's first photographer. Exhibitions of her work have been staged in more than fifty galleries worldwide. She has been voted the USA's Female Photographer of the Year, and has published four books of photography.

DAVID MAGNUS

David Magnus was still in his late teens when he took the pictures of Jimi outside Chas Chandler's flat into which the guitarist and Kathy Etchingham had just moved. "I was just an up and coming youngster, eager to take pictures of who I could, when I could and to sell them for what I could. Jimi was sweet and charming, but all I really remember about the session was how bloody cold it was!" Magnus still takes photographs, for Rex Features, and lives in Middlesex.

GERED MANKOWITZ

Gered was born in London in 1946, left school at fifteen and was offered an apprenticeship at Camera Press. He began work in fashion photography before shooting his first record sleeve in 1963, eventually opening a studio in London. His first shoot with Marianne Faithfull led to a further commission from her manager to portray his other group, Tthe Rolling Stones: he photographed them for several album sleeves. For thirty years, Gered has photographed the most celebrated figures in popular culture; he has also moved into advertising, book covers and movie stills. In 1982 Mankowitz staged an exhibition at the Photographer's Gallery which went on to tour Britain for two years. Now working from north London, Mankowitz contributes to selected major publications, and is a recipient of many prestigious awards.

Cover: Gered Mankowitz / David Costa "Purple and Gold" limited edition silk screen. Bowstir Ltd, P.O.Box 7556, London, NW3 2LH.

MOEBIUS

Jean "Moebius" Giraud has influenced an entire generation of fantasy artists. Born in 1938, Giraud sold his first cartoon strip, a western, when he was seventeen. In the late 1960s, working under the alias of Moebius, he began working for the hugely influential French publication, *Metal Hurlant* (Heavy Metal), which changed the face of European comic art. After being asked to work on the film *Alien*, he designed for a diverse range of clients, including Citroën, Credit Agricole, and Greenpeace. He has subsequently been involved with the movies *Willow, Nemo, Masters Of The Universe, The Abyss* and *TRON*. Jean Giraud divides his time between his homes in Paris and Los Angeles.

Art : Martin Monestier / Central Image : Joseph Sia

ARE YOU EXPERIENCED?
Words and Music
by JIMI HENDRIX

MARTIN MONESTIER

Author, collagist and graphic artist, Martin Monestier's collage of Jimi is one of a series - which includes the composer Mozart - that the Parisian has recently completed.

VICTOR MOSCOSO

A transplanted New Yorker, Moscoso was one of the few West Coast psychedelic artists with extensive formal training. A co-founder of ZAP Comix, his deliberate use of almost illegible lettering was designed to grab the public's attention. He worked occasionally with Rick Griffin; their design for *The Beetle* amply illustrates the expanse of their comic book art and is a rare example of their collaborative work.

MICHAEL OCHS ARCHIVES

Michael Ochs is considered the foremost music archivist in the United States. His research services, the Michael Ochs Archives, are used extensively worldwide, supplying photographs, music props and data for movies, television productions, periodicals, record reissue packages and books. After managing the career of his brother, noted folk singer Phil Ochs, he then headed the public relations department at Columbia Records, Shelter Records, and ABC Records. In the mid 1970s he established the Michael Ochs Archives. Among the Archives' vast resources are the complete photographic works of famed celebrity photographers James Kriegsmann, Ray Whitten, Steve Paley and Earl Leaf as well as the negatives and transparencies shot for such classic magazines as *Hit Parader, Tiger Beat, Right On, Song Hits* and *Rona Barrett's Hollywood*.

ROB O'CONNOR : STYLOROUGE

Rob O'Connor studied Graphic Design at Brighton Art College in the late 1970s before becoming art director at Polydor Records in 1979. He quit in 1981 to work in a one-room office in west London with no furniture and a borrowed telephone. From such inauspicious beginnings Stylorouge has built up an enviable reputation as an established design unit within the leisure industry. Book, fashion and video projects run alongside design and art direction for record covers, posters and corporate advertisements. Rob O'Connor is one of the pioneering members of the Association of Music Industry Designers, which represents the interests of designers working in the music industry. Stylorouge works for clients from all over Europe, Japan and North America.

IVAN OLIVIER

Ivan Olivier designed the artwork for the French-only release of *All Along The Watchtower*.

RICHARD PETERS

Richard Peters illustrated the sleeve for Jimi's posthumously released *Crash Landing* record.

MIKE POLILLO

San Francisco-based Mike Polillo photographed Jimi Hendrix at the Panhandle, a week after Jimi had played Monterey. Both his images in this book started life as black and white prints which have been subsequently hand coloured.

DÖLF PREISIG

Swiss-based Dölf Preisig photographed Hendrix and the other acts - Traffic, John Mayall, Eric Burdon and others - who played in Zurich at the Hallenstadion in 1968. Journalist Keith Altham who covered the shows recalls, "What a plane-load that was! The plane flew at 18,000 feet, the crew and passengers were at 24,000!"

RON RAFAELLI

Los Angeles-based Rafaelli spent a month on the road with Hendrix and the Experience in 1968 on the West Coast and on vacation in Hawaii, detailing their life on and off stage. Rafaelli also had a predilection for girls in pictures and, if he could persuade them to take some of their clothes off so much the better (hence the Electric Ladies image). *Electric Church / A Visual Experience*, a book of his pictures, was sold on the group's 1969 American tour. While most of the black and white images survive, all of the colour is thought lost.

JEAN LOUIS RANCUREL

Jean Louis Rancurel was born in Paris in 1946 and became seconded to the first French rock magazine, *Disco Revue*, in 1961. Jean Louis' first pictures - of Gene Vincent - were taken at L'Etoile in Paris. He became senior photographer at *Disco Revue* in 1966, shooting all of the prominent musicians of the day and also worked freelance for a variety of record companies and TV shows. Currently, Jean Louis runs Phototheque Rancurel in Paris; his pictures have been syndicated throughout Europe, the United States, Scandinavia and Japan.

RUSH AND BLAM

Rush and Blam studied design on Venus. Cheap Northern Labour. One 'O' level between them.

CHRIS SALEWICZ

Chris Salewicz has documented world popular culture for over two decades, both in print and on television. His writing, on subjects from film to foreign affairs, has appeared in the *Sunday Times,* the *Independent, Q,* the *Face,* the *Los Angeles Times* and the *Sydney Morning Herald*, and in many other publications worldwide. As a senior features writer for *NME* from 1975 to 1981, he saw service at the frontlines of glam rock, punk rock, and reggae music Among the highlights, he visited the Gun Court with Bob Marley when he went to plead for the life of a condemned man. In 1978 he was assistant director of *DOA*, the definitive US film about punk rock. He was a contributing editor of *Time Out*, worked for the *Sunday Times Magazine*, and provided two of the cover stories in issue one of Q. A founder member of MTV Europe, he presented Kino, a weekly 60 minute pan-European film magazine programme from 1987-1989. He has subsequently directed artists as varied as Sting and the Senegalese musician Baaba Maal. His books include *McCartney, the Definitive Biography*, published by St Martin's in 1986; *Midnights In Moscow* (with Adrian Boot), a travel guide to perestroika based on a trip round the Soviet Union with Billy Bragg; and *Bob Marley, Songs Of Freedom* (with Adrian Boot), the authorised-by-the-estate biography published worldwide on February 6, 1995, the fiftieth anniversary of the birth of Bob Marley. Chris Salewicz works best when he has had a lot of sleep.

CHARLES SHAAR MURRAY

Charles Shaar Murray won the *Rolling Stone*-sponsored Ralph J. Gleason Music Book Award for *Crosstown Traffic: Jimi Hendrix and Postwar Pop* (Faber & Faber, 1989). A contributor to the notorious 1970 OZ Schoolkids' issue and former associate editor of the *New Musical Express*, his journalism, criticism, wild theorising and vulgar abuse have also appeared in *Q, Vogue*, *Rolling Stone*, the *Observer* and the *Guardian*, and he currently pontificates on a variety of topics for the *Daily Telegraph, New Statesman, MacUser, Guitar World, Mojo* and *Time Out*. In 1991, Penguin Books published *Shots From The Hip*, a selection of his journalism, criticism, theorising, abuse etc., and by the time you read this he may even have completed *The Boogie Man*, his long-awaited biography of John Lee Hooker.

MARTIN SHARP

Martin Sharp was born in 1942 and graduated from Sydney University in 1961. He was art director for the trailblazing *OZ* magazine in both Australia and London as well as contributor to the *Sydney Morning Herald*, *Australian* and *Honi Soit*. From 1966-1970 Martin worked in London for Big O Posters. He designed for, among others, Cream; he created their *Disraeli Gears* and *Wheels Of Fire* album sleeves and many memorable posters - he also wrote the lyrics to their song, "Tales Of Brave Ulysses." Sharp's poster of Jimi Hendrix was enormously important. Sharp was art adviser for the movie *Picnic At Hanging Rock* and has staged numerous one-man exhibitions throughout Australia. Martin Sharp was awarded the Queen Elizabeth Jubilee Medal in 1977.

JOSEPH SIA

Noted photographer Joseph Sia covered innumerable Jimi Hendrix shows. Included in this book are images from Yale University, the Atlanta Pop Festival on Independence Day, 1970, and the Band Of Gypsys' debut in New York in 1969.

ARNOLD SKOLNIK

Arnold Skolnik designed the final version of the Woodstock poster. The original design by David Byrd went through a variety of permutations as new variants on the poster had to be created as artists were added to the bill.

LUCIA SOLAZZI

Lucia began an interest in astrology while living in France. Born of Italian parents in Morocco, Lucia has always been interested in the esoteric sciences. She is now a certified teacher of yoga and lives in Los Angeles.

NEIL SPENCER

Neil Spencer is a writer and journalist. Formerly editor of the *New Musical Express* during that paper's most successful era, he has also served time as assistant editor of Arena men's magazine and is a founding editor of *Straight No Chaser*, the magazine of world jazz jive. Currently he is music critic with the *Observer*. A teenage Saturday job in Burton's the tailors established his fascination with clothes; his essay on "Menswear In The Eighties" appears in *Chic Thrills, A Fashion Reader* (Pandora).

ROGER STEFFENS

Roger Steffens served in Vietnam for the last twenty-six months of the 1960s, working primarily with refugees, and doing a weekly TV show reading poetry to the combat troops. He is the founding editor of the *[Reggae and African] Beat* Magazine, and edits its annual Bob Marley Collectors' Edition. His articles and photographs have appeared in *Rolling Stone, Musician, Village Voice, New York Times, Los Angeles Times, High Times* and in France, Sweden, Finland, Italy, Japan and Canada. A professional actor since 1965, Steffens has appeared in films and television (most recently *Forrest Gump*) and is the narrator of an Oscar-winning documentary.

WALDEMAR SWIERZY

Swierzy was born in 1931 in Katowice, Poland. He graduated from the Cracow Academy of Fine Art and has been a freelance graphic and poster designer ever since. He is author of more than one thousand posters. He won the Toulouse-Lautrec Grand Prix in 1959, first prize at the Prix X Biennale di Sao Paolo in 1970 and the gold medal in the International Poster Biennale in Warsaw six years later. In 1975 and 1985 he won first prize in *Hollywood Reporter's* annual film poster competition. He has had exhibitions all over the world including Tokyo, Copenhagen, Caracas and Moscow. Since 1965 he has been Professor in the Higher School of Fine Arts in Poznan and is a member of the Alliance Graphique Internationale.

DEREK TAYLOR

Derek Taylor sees himself as an optimistic boy from the *Hoylake and West Kirby Advertiser* who got lucky, met a beautiful girl from Birkenhead, fell in love, got married forever and lives happily in paradise in a watermill on the Stour in Suffolk. Long ago and far away he met and served the Beatles - still does, in a way - and went on to star in two comedy-dramas based on the music business with Warner Bros, in London and Los Angeles in the 1970s. He dropped out, with his vocabulary, hair and sobriety intact and now works as a freelance in between experiments with herbal medicine He and his wife Joan have three daughters, three sons and three (rising four) grandchildren.

BRUNO TILLEY

Bruno Tilley graduated from St Martins School of Art in London in 1979. Tilley joined Island Records the following year as in-house designer and within four years had assumed the role of creative director for the company. In his ten years with Island he was responsible for setting up Island Art, heading a nine-strong team to design all aspects of promotional material. Bruno also commissioned and directed many of the company's promotional videos. He is the recipient of numerous awards for sleeves, posters and videos; in 1986 he scooped the top four awards for Consumer Advertising Design in the prestigious *Music Week*. Since 1990, Bruno Tilley has headed his own design company, Mainline Productions, which is based in London.

ART TROITSKY

Born in Moscow in 1955, Art Troitsky spent his childhood in Prague, where his father was a diplomat, before returning to live in the Soviet capital when he was a teenager. There he first became a DJ, before turning to rock journalism in the late 1970s. He was also an independent entrepreneur and underground networker, promoting New Wave Soviet rock. In the early 1980s he wrote for official publications and illegal fanzines, and in 1984, after suggesting a more liberal attitude towards the burgeoning rise of the Soviet rock movement, his writing was officially banned. In 1986, however, he became the organiser of the concert for the victims of the Chernobyl disaster. Rescued by Glasnost, Troitsky is now involved in numerous enterprises, employed by Soviet TV as a writer and presenter, and travels the world negotiating deals for video-rights, among other matters. Troitsky's first book, *Back In The USSR* (Omnibus), was published in 1987, and has since been translated into seven different languages. In 1990 he published the first encyclopaedia of Soviet rock, and the same year his *Tu Sovka* (Who's Who in The New Soviet Rock Culture) was published in Britain. Troitsky is involved with *Glas* (Voice), a Moscow-based international arts magazine, and is the Moscow correspondent for *Rolling Stone*. He is also editor-in-chief of the Russian edition of *Playboy*.

BERND WEIDEMANN

A communication design graduate from Hamburg, Bernd Weidemann began etching work on Hendrix while still a student. In his art he tries to visualise the musical feeling and structure of Jimi's songs in one single medium, etching.

Paparazzi. Photograph : Elliott Landy

1968: Shot at the Copter Club in the Pan Am Building in New York at the end of the British Are Coming press conference. Organised by Michael Goldstein, Jimi's American PR, the newly arrived British groups were supposed to land next to the Copter Club by helicopter but the stunt misfired due to the lousy weather conditions. Besides his upcoming tour which would take him to Seattle for the first time in many years, Jimi was also supposed to be promoting his new album, Axis: Bold As Love. *Somewhat noncommittal about the record which would go on to spend some fifty-three weeks on the US chart, Jimi offered a few telling observations to the assembled hacks that his family still didn't really know much about the level of success he was enjoying.*

VAL WILMER

Born in Harrogate, Yorkshire, Val Wilmer began photographing visiting American jazz musicians with her mother's box Brownie while still at school. Her deep involvement with the music remained as she travelled widely to shoot and interview giants such as Duke Ellington, Muddy Waters and Ornette Coleman and unknown blues players in the deep south. By the time she photographed Jimi Hendrix, she was a regular at TV rehearsals for *Ready Steady Go!*. but already tired of hackneyed 'action' shots. For her, the musicians have always been about far more than what they did on stage, and she set out to capture these other dimensions whenever possible. Widely published and with work in four major permanent collections, she lives in north London with a marmalade cat named Sam, and once gave Jimi Hendrix a lift in her car.

IAN WRIGHT

A self-confessed painter and decorator, south Londoner Ian Wright's vivid interpretations of sound and fury first found their home in the pages of *NME* where his vision of any new album would be scanned with as much curiosity as the reviewer's verdict. Since then, Ian has composed sleeve art for Pete Townshend, King Sunny Ade, Madness, Black Uhuru, he has worked regularly for Island Records, Talkin' Loud and Adrian Sherwood's ON-U Sound label. His work can be viewed regularly in *Straight No Chaser* magazine, *Esquire,* the *Guardian* and the *Sunday Times.*

SUE YOUNG

Sue Young has been a director of animation since the beginning of the 1980s. Her credits range from work with such clients as Budweiser to the BBC, for whom she made the One World title sequence, to Bob Marley's Time Will Tell documentary. Among much other work, she also helped create MTV's state-of-the-art graphics and made *The Doomsday Clock*, a disarmament film for the United Nations. In 1992 she animated Jimi Hendrix's "Fire" when it was released as a single. Her awards include Best Animation at the 1985 Annecy Animation Festival and gold and silver medals at the 1993 New York International Advertising Awards

Space Imagery courtesy of NASA

Electronic Imaging: Exhibit-A. Technical Support: Leeds Photovisual

© Copyright Credits

Al Hendrix: p22
Allan Koss: p242
Arnold Skolnik - Woodstock Ventures: p240
AYEI: p92; p232
Bernd Wiedemann: p38; p39; p41
BGP Archives: p208; p209; p211
Bruno Tilley: p87
Caesar Glebbeek: p177
Caroline Coon: p149; p158
David Magnus - Rex Features: p62; p147; p194; p198
Dezo Hoffman: p174
Dölf Preisig: p230
Douglas Kent Hall: p27; p123; p145
Ed Caraeff: p140
Elliott Landy: p154
Exhibit-A: p10; p175
Gered Mankowitz: p71; p72; p76
Gered Mankowitz - David Costa: p4; p75; p77; p171; p173
Graham Howe - Camera Press: p37
Ian Wright: p18; p136; p181; p236
Ira Cohen: p84; p85
Ivan Oliver: p57
AYEI: p218
Jean Noel Coghe: p83; p132
Jean Pierre Leloir: p42; p43; p125; p186; p187; p191; p205
Joel Axelrad - Retna: p65; p45; p126
Joseph Sia: p34; p215; p227; p247
John Adler: p103
Linda McCartney: p32; p49; p184; p185; p235
Lucia Solazzi / John O'Brian: p95
Mark French / Bill Wood: p207
AYEI / Martin Monestier / Central Image-Joseph Sia: p149; p151
Martin Sharp: p55; p56
Mati Klarwein: p51
Michael Ochs Archives: p46; p68; p80; p150; p151; p162; p163; p178; p193
Mike Polillo: p216
Mobius: p3; p83
Prof. Gunther Kieser: p212
Rancurel - Lampard: p78; p79; p111; p161; p164
Richard Baker - IQ: p28
AYEI: p90
Richard Peters: p88
Rob O'Connor - Stylorouge / Pictor-Uniphoto: p119
Robert Knight: p183
Ron Rafaelli - Michael Ochs Archives: p15; p17; p30; p98; p99; p130; p131; p152; p153; p156; p157; p188
Roz Kelly - Michael Ochs Archives: p67
Rush and Blam: p223
Sue Young: p166; p167
Terence Donovan: p168
Val Wilmer: p109; p201
Waldemar Swierzy: p114; p115

GET EXPERIENCED!

ARE

YOU EXPERIENCED?